The Translator's Handbook
by
Frederick Fuller

The bibliography of translation today is vast, sophisticated, and, for the reader with a scholarly turn of mind, utterly absorbing. But try to cull from among the learned volumes on the history, the theory, the science, the analysis, the strategies, of translation something that will be of immediate, practical use to the translator who is busy working on an economic report or a political speech, and you will almost certainly return empty-handed. Then look round for books with a more empirical, every-day approach to the subject, and again you are likely to find that, as the author of this *Handbook* discovered: "practical hints on the tricks of the translation trade are not easy to come by".

The Translator's Handbook is intended to be just that — a *vade-mecum* for daily use, to be kept within easy reach. The old hand momentarily at a loss may find just the right synonym among the selection offered. The less experienced but eager translator will find here in addition a wealth of information on the day-to-day problems of turning French and Spanish into English, written in an easy, readable style that imparts instruction without appearing to do so.

Frederick Fuller studied Romance and Germanic philology with such eminent scholars as Allison Peers in Liverpool, Karl Vossler in Munich, Joseph Bédier at the Sorbonne, André Morize and Jeremiah Ford at Harvard. He was for some years Assistant Keeper at the British Library, and he worked as Language Supervisor in the BBC during the War and as British Council lecturer and music officer in Brazil, Argentina and Chile. His translations include *The Enlargement of the European Communities* (Puissochet) from French; *Stravinsky* (Vlad) from Italian; libretti and other musical texts, and poetry, into French, Spanish and Portuguese, and from these and many other languages, including the Scandinavian languages and Russian, into English.

THE TRANSLATOR'S HANDBOOK

THE TRANSLATOR'S HANDBOOK

(with special reference to conference translation from French and Spanish)

Frederick Fuller, M.A.

Sometime Senior Reviser, United Nations

THE PENNSYLVANIA STATE UNIVERSITY PRESS

University Park

Copyright © 1973, 1984 by Frederick Fuller

Published in Great Britain by Colin Smythe Ltd.

Published in the United States of America by
The Pennsylvania State University Press

Library of Congress Cataloging in Publication Data

Fuller, Frederick
   The translator's handbook.

   1. Translating and interpreting. I. Title.
   P306.F8   1984   418'.02   83-22107
   ISBN 0-271-00368-5

Produced in Great Britain

CONTENTS

7

Note for the American and Canadian User

Since this edition of the *Handbook* is being printed both for Colin Smythe Limited and for the Pennsylvania State University Press, it might seem desirable, or at least courteous, to adopt American spelling, terminology, etc., for the copies to be sold in the United States. But even if it were practicable I think it would be a mistake. The world's leading employer of translators — the United Nations — for historical reasons uses "British" English in all its publications. So, I would imagine, do the majority of international organizations outside the American continent. In any case, the international conference translator has to be equipped to switch over from one set of practices to the other at a moment's notice, and no doubt the constant use of this *Handbook* will help in some small measure to make the American translator more aware of the everyday differences, most of them superficial ones, in English usage on both sides of the Atlantic. When I myself work in Washington for the Pan American Health Organization or the State Department, I have to make the same changeover from one day to the next, and long practice makes it no more difficult than switching over from right-hand to left-hand driving.

F.F.

Foreword

In the Introduction to the first edition of this *Handbook*, I described it as "an unpretentious *farrago* of odds and ends rather than a treatise on the art of translation". Perhaps odds and ends are a commodity that appeals to the translator mind, because to my surprise and delight, the book was flatteringly reviewed in the specialist journals and — what is far more important — gratifyingly well received by the translating profession. It is now used as a textbook in universities and schools of translation throughout the world, with the result that it has gone out of print. For lack of time, I was tempted to ask the publisher simply to reprint the first edition as it stands; but since I am constantly being asked to expand the scope of the *Handbook*, I decided to respond in some small measure at least by adding a Part II devoted to translation from the second most important language, in terms of volume, for international conference work, namely Spanish.

Apart from that, I have relented somewhat from my expressed reluctance "to spare the translator the trouble of selecting the best equivalent of any given word or phrase". There is, after all, no real escape from that chore anyway, and there is perhaps some virtue in suggesting alternatives that may encourage the translator not to be satisfied with the first rendering that suggests itself. I still feel that the most valuable parts of the book are the longer, general headings: *Ambiguity*, *Dialogue*, *Imagination*, *Jargon*, etc., which without actually claiming to do so embody general principles of translation, and I am still not tempted by the notion of grouping these headings in a separate section, logical though that may be. But I have tried to be of some slight assistance to the reader by sifting through these longer headings and extracting — and adding as a postlude — such general elements of good translation as they contain. This is not Horace's *monumentum aere perennius*; it is a tentative decalogue to be weighed, amplified, added to or subtracted from at will, but above all practised.

Otherwise Part I of the original *Handbook* remains largely as it stood. A number of new entries have been added and alterations made to existing entries, but I have not been obliged to make any deletions on grounds of inaccuracy. Whether this means that there was no fault to be found with it or that critics did not take the trouble to point out shortcomings, as I invited them to do, I cannot say. There are two minor changes. First (see *First, firstly* in Part I), the interleaving in the earlier edition — unnumbered blank sheets — seems to have inhibited some users, who actually inserted additions and comments on the printed page rather than sully the virgin sheets facing the texts. This time a number of pages have been inserted at the end of each Part, lined and marked NOTES. Secondly, I have added "M.A." after my name. To quote one's academic qualifications seemed to me something only appropriate for writers of school textbooks. But having been undeservedly elevated by some of my readers to the ranks of that rare company of great autodidacts, including Disraeli, Bernard Shaw, Fred Hoyle, E. V. Pritchett *et al.*, who have bypassed the university and achieved eminence without it, I have humbly to confess that I attended not one but four universities, in four different countries. However, since as I have said the Handbook is after all being used as a textbook, perhaps the mention may be appropriate.

Frederick Fuller,
February 1984

Introduction
to the First English Edition (1973)

In the course of many years as English reviser for the United Nations in New York, Geneva, Santiago (Chile), and at international conferences all over the world, I have been in the habit of jotting down on index cards examples of what I considered to be good or bad translation practice that recurred frequently in documents I revised. I had hoped at some convenient time to study the material systematically with a view to publishing a general work on translation, and I still hope to do this one day.

In the meantime it occurred to me that since the bulk of the material I had collected deals with problems of immediate concern to the growing army of international conference translators rather than to the translator of technical treatises or of fiction or biography or poetry, it might be useful to publish it with the conference translator particularly in mind.

This explains certain features of the present Handbook which might otherwise seem odd. It has been suggested, for example, that the larger or more general headings such as *"Style"*, *"Jargon"*, etc. might more logically be grouped together at the beginning. But what I had in mind was an unpretentious *farrago* of odds and ends rather than a treatise on the art of translation, and the strictly alphabetical form has its own logic which I think must take precedence. It is convenient to have alternative renderings of terms that recur frequently in international conference vocabulary and are notoriously difficult to translate, arranged in the form of a short glossary.

But I do not regard this as the most valuable part of the Handbook. It was not my intention to spare the translator the trouble of selecting the best equivalent of any given word or phrase. If he finds himself at a loss for a good translation of, say, *"illusoire"* and can find exactly what he wants here under that word, so much the better; but if in the process his eye catches the next heading *"Imagination"*, and he is sufficiently intrigued to read it, my purpose will to that extent have been served. If I may quote myself on the subject: "Perhaps the main purpose of this Handbook is to try to bring home to translators the danger of falling into a dull routine and the need for keeping the mind fresh and alert." For similar reasons I have not always given examples where they might have elucidated the points made. It is often difficult to illustrate a point adequately by means of a single example; and since the Handbook is intended mainly for professional translators, I have in many cases assumed that they will recognize the point I am making, and keep a lookout when they come across words or phrases or constructions I have noted as containing booby-traps or as being otherwise of special interest.

Many of the longer headings overlap: examples of *Gallicisms* could obviously be entered equally well under *Translatorese*; *Dialogue* could be incorporated into *Jargon*, and so on. But I have resisted the temptation to deprive the compilation of its 'unconsidered trifles' character, in the hope that what it loses in *rigueur scientifique* it makes up in readability.

The Handbook embodies the results of many valuable criticisms made by my former colleagues; where I have found them acceptable, the text has been modified accordingly. But quite frequently I have persisted in my views in spite of a considerable weight of opinion on the other side. Indeed at times I have been deliberately provocative, in the hope that my opinions will produce some reaction in the reader, if only of exasperation. It is the easiest thing in the world for the conference translator, once he has acquired the knack, to turn out semi-automatic translations which will just about pass muster but leave much to be desired. To quote again from the text under *"Imagination"*: "Staleness is an occupational disease

12

of the translator"; and if anything I have to say can provide a stimulus, of whatever kind, there is an even chance that translation work will be the better for it.

The original glossary on which this Handbook is based included entries in French, Spanish, Portuguese, German, Swedish and Russian; but since French is by far the most important language from which English-speaking translators have to work in the international organizations, and since the principles discussed under the more general headings apply to translation from any language, the entries relating to the other languages have been omitted from the present edition.

Many of the users of this *vade-mecum* will no doubt be translators whom I have met or will meet at international conferences around the world. I shall not take it amiss if they buttonhole me in the corridors or write to me at the address given below, and put me right where I have gone wrong. Indeed, I shall welcome any comments, favourable or unfavourable, that will help to make any subsequent edition more useful.

F.F.

Manor Barn
Ratton Village
Eastbourne
Sussex, England

PART I

TRANSLATING FROM FRENCH INTO ENGLISH

Important Explanatory Note

The indications *"Not . . . But . . ."* are not necessarily intended to be categorical. In some cases they merely suggest that the first term is less acceptable than the second.

The letters (E), (F) are placed after words spelt alike in English and French, to indicate which language is to be understood.

A

Absence (F)

L'absence de moyens de transport adéquats. Not "absence"
But "The fact that no . . . were available", "the lack of".
"Absence" here not only has a French ring, but carries a
suggestion of *temporary* lack. (See *Gallicisms, Translatorese,
Présence.*)

Abstract nouns

Good English usually prefers the concrete to the abstract.
To say "effect the solution of a problem" instead of "solve it"
adds nothing to the sense and detracts from the style.

Sous prétexte de l'existence d'un complot. Not ". . . of the
existence of a plot" *But* "that there was a plot".

Le problème posé par l'accroissement des fournitures . . .:
"The problem of increasing the supply . . ."

Abuser

Pour ne pas abuser de votre patience. Not "So as not to abuse
your patience" *But* ". . . not to try your patience". (See
Translatorese.)

Actually

A very useful word for giving emphasis (see *En effet*).

Adapté à

"Adapted to" often smacks of translatorese (q.v.). "Suitable
for, in keeping with," etc., will be generally preferable. ". . .

permettrait de définir une politique qui serait adaptée aux besoins des pays . . . *Not* "which would be adapted to . . ." (adapted or adjusted by whom?) *But* ". . . a policy . . . appropriate to the needs of . . .". "Matched, matching, consonant with, in keeping with", etc. are other possibilities. If, exceptionally, *"Time Magazine* style" is called for, "tailored to, geared to" may be appropriate.

Adhérer, adhésion
In treaties and similar instruments, *Not* "adhere, adhesion" *But* "accede, accession".

Afin de
Where it is uncertain whether the result will be achieved, "with a view to" is often preferable to "in order to", e.g. . . . *conversations tenues afin de signer un contrat.*

Agit (Il s'agit)
Some alternatives to the obvious translation "it is a matter of", which recalls the schoolroom: "the point (aim, idea, intention, object, point at issue) is; what is wanted is; the feature to note is; . . . is involved, is at stake." Cf. also . . . *un autre fait important. Il s'agit de* . . . *Not* "Another important matter. It relates to . . .", *But* "Another important matter is . . .".

Ainsi que
This is frequently used in French merely to avoid a succession of words joined together by *"et"*, e.g. *Les architectes et les médecins font défaut, ainsi que les hommes de science.* If the *ainsi que* is translated by "as well as", it may suggest a difference of emphasis not intended in the French, where its purpose is often merely stylistic. Hence it may be better to translate it simply as "and".

Ajouter
Reports of speeches in French frequently use *"il ajoute que"* when there is no suggestion of an afterthought or an incidental

remark such as "he added that" implies. "He went on to say, furthermore there was . . ., he also considered", or some such phrase will often give the sense more precisely. In many cases the phrase can be ignored.

Altération

For the pejorative implication of this word, see Harrap's *French-English Dictionary*; also Part II: *Alteración*.

Ambiguity

Certain words lead very easily to ambiguity in written English, and various devices have to be used to supply the stress given to them in speech. Conference translators must be particularly alive to this, since a large proportion of their work is based on texts intended to be spoken.

Il pense, lui aussi, que Not "he also believed" (he also? or also believed?) *But* "he too believed".

Le Président prie . . . de ne plus faire d'observations personnelles Not "not to make any more personal remarks" (more personal? or more remarks?) *But* "To refrain from making (any further) . . ."; "not to continue to make . . .".

"Unless more properly trained people are available" (more people? or more properly trained? If the latter is meant, "better trained" would avoid the ambiguity.

On ne peut néanmoins sous-estimer la gravité . . . Not "cannot be" *But* "must (should) not be". No doubt the original is ambiguous, but the translator is after all expected to render the thought. It makes sense to say that something "cannot be overestimated" but when the writer here says *"on ne peut"*, he presumably means "it would be unthinkable or unreasonable to".

The use of "e.g." instead of "for example" can often help to avoid ambiguity. In the sentence: "There are refugees professionally trained, for example, artisans, technicians . . ." the "for example" can look both ways, so that it is impossible to be sure whether the "professionally trained" refers to the "artisans etc." or whether the latter represent additional categories. "There are . . ., e.g. artisans, . . ." clears up the point.

". . . old regulations. Their abolition is advocated as being inefficient." (What is inefficient — the regulations or the abolition?)

". . . had clearly explained his Government's position" (obviously? or in a clear manner?).

"It had handed over half to the Agency" (handed over? or over half?).

Les propriétés en jeu Not "the property entailed" (estate in fee tail?) *But* "involved, concerned, in question".

Toutes les guerres ne sont pas interdites par la Charte Not "All wars are not forbidden" *But* "Not all wars are forbidden". The former sentence is not clear without the spoken stress on "all".

"Both the facts mentioned and those referred to . . ." (the two facts?). Say "Not only the facts . . . but . . .". (See also *Both*.)

Comme pour les veaux vivants, les importations de gros bovins . . . If we say "As for live calves . . .", we are translating *"Quant aux . . ."* Say "Just as for", or "In the case of" (but see also *Case*!).

Un institut qui possède une instruction organisée: Not "which has organized instruction" (*qui a organisé*) *But* "which provides, which arranges for . . .".

Amené à
See *Appelé à*.

Analyse (E)
Analyser in French is to "study, consider", even "summarize". "Analyse" (E) suggests a more thorough examination than the French usually implies.

And which
English has a number of neat ways of avoiding the unpleasing concatenation of clauses joined together by "which . . . and which", e.g. "A list of projects which were in various stages of preparation and which would have". *Better*: "projects in various stages of preparation which . . .". *Les intérêts d'un*

autre Etat qui vient d'accéder à l'indépendance et qui ne fait pas partie du continent. Say "another newly-independent State not situated . . .". French does not appear to object to the combination of a participle and an "and which" clause in a sentence like: *"Une somme déposée à la banque et qui se retire ensuite".* In English the constructions should correspond: participle . . . participle, or "which . . . and which", but the latter is best avoided as suggested above.

Annex

Reproduit en annexe. Not "in the annex" *(dans l'annexe) But* "annexed (appended) hereto", "attached", or "as an annex" (where the matter constitutes the entire annex).

Appelé à

"Led to" is seldom a satisfactory translation. "How . . . came to, destined to (for), earmarked for, marked out for, expected to, meant to, supposed to, having to, responsible for", are a few of the many ways in which translators can avoid the humdrum, line-of-least-resistance version. *Appelé à d'autres fonctions:* "assigned to . . .".

Approximate

Note that "British" English says: To approximate *to* something. American English omits the preposition.

Archaisms

Archaic words like "anent, for the nonce", perhaps even "albeit", are seldom appropriate in conference work. "Archaic words thrust into a commonplace text to redeem its ordinariness are an abomination" (Fowler).

Aspect

French tends to use this word in a vacuum, with little or no reference to the matter to which the "aspect" relates. (Spanish goes even further: *En este aspecto* is often used meaning simply "in this respect".) Translators should try not to leave the word "aspect" dangling in the air. *"Cet aspect doit être étudié de près*: "This aspect of the matter (problem, etc.) calls for close attention."

Aspirations
Where this word is used of people aspiring to a better life, etc., "aspirations" or "ideals" may be the best rendering. But it is often used in relation to the attainment of a more specific and mundane goal, and it would then be better rendered by "desires, hopes, wishes, what . . . wants, what . . . has in mind, target, ambitions, goals," etc. (See *Translatorese.*)

Assurer
Le gouvernement tient à assurer le transport entre . . . ". . . to provide transport . . .". *Assurer* is often a slightly more elegant variation (q.v.) of *faire*: Assurer la liaison entre . . ." "make, establish a link between . . .

As to, as for
Many people feel that "as for" carries with it a slightly deprecatory suggestion. (See *Nuance.*)

Attitudes
The plural in English may suggest ballet dancing, and the singular is usually better. The word can sometimes be omitted entirely, e.g. *Mais quelle que soit la motivation de ces attitudes, il faut espérer. Not* "whatever the motivation of these attitudes" *But* "whatever the (underlying) motives".

Aussi
As every schoolboy should know, *aussi* with inversion of the following verb and subject does *Not* mean "also", *But* "and therefore, hence, accordingly", etc.

D'autant plus que
The obvious rendering "the more so as", etc., sometimes makes poor English. Alternatives are "inasmuch as, especially as, particularly as, because, *a fortiori*", etc.

Auteurs
Of a resolution: "Sponsors".

Avis
Après avis conforme. Not "on the strength of an opinion to that effect" *But* "with the concurrence of", or ". . . concurring, with the consent of", etc.

B

Base
Se baser (fonder) sur. S'inspirer de. Not "base themselves on", which has a Gallic sound, *But* "base their policy, actions, etc., on".

Before
Make sure when translating sentences like ' *il se réserve (le droit) de prendre la parole devant l'Assemblée* ' as "to speak before the Assembly" that the context does not allow of the interpretation "before the Assembly met" (i.e. *"avant la session de l'Assemblée"*). Cf. "His delegation had drafted the resolution before the Assembly." What does it mean? (See *Ambiguity*.)

Bien-fondé
Le bien-fondé de sa proposition: the merit, virtue, justification (in a particular context), soundness. (See also *Translatorese.*)

Both
Ces deux dispositions sont inconciliables. Not "Both these . . ." *But* "The two . . .". *"Both"* here would suggest that each one, take separately, is irreconcilable, whereas obviously the meaning is that the one is irreconcilable with the other.

Both . . . and
This construction is very frequently misused (see *Grammar*).

23

The rule is given neatly by Gowers *(ABC of English Usage)*: ". . . any word or words common to both the items joined by these conjunctions must either be repeated after each or taken *outside* and put in front of 'both'. Thus you can say 'both for eating and for drinking' or 'for both eating and drinking', but not 'both for eating and drinking'." A similar principle applies to "not only . . . but also" (see *Grammar*, fifth example).

Brackets

It may be worth noting that American English differentiates between brackets = [   ] and parentheses = (   ). "British" English calls them square and round brackets respectively. In British usage, a "parenthesis" does not necessarily use brackets at all — commas or dashes may be used; hence it is safer, in Europe at any rate, to use the term "square brackets" and "round brackets".

Since conference translating often involves a certain amount of "editing" for publication, it is useful for translators to have some acquaintance with standard editorial practices. One of these is that if the end part of a sentence is enclosed in brackets, the full stop comes after the bracket, e.g. "I shall come (if I can)." But if an entire sentence is placed within brackets, the bracket follows the full stop, the principle being that if the matter enclosed within the brackets is removed, the passage can stand, e.g. "The report is reproduced below (see annex II)." *But* "The report is reproduced below. (See annex II.)"

Brillant

Le brillant discours de M. . . . "Brilliant" is a word to be used reluctantly in conference work. "Excellent, able" will often sound less fulsome, *Brillante élection* may mean "(almost) unanimous, overwhelming, outstanding(-ly successful), impressive", . . . *brillamment exposé par . . .*: "skilfully, ably, outlined by . . .", "the masterly account given by . . .".

The translator must remember the tendency in certain languages to use superlatives, and the consequent need to tone down the language used so as to reproduce the meaning rather than the words. "Brilliant" may of course be just the word needed, but some more modified rapture may render the thought more accurately. *Briller* = excel.

British

Not "British law" *But* "English law" (and "American law" if this is included). "Anglo-Saxon law" is sometimes used by contrast with "Roman law", to indicate any system derived from common law.

Brutal (F)

". . . *viole ces accords de la manière la plus brutale.* A literal translation sometimes sounds more melodramatic than the original French. Perhaps "ruthless, outrageous" would provide alternatives.

C

Cadre

Dans le cadre de. Do not automatically resort to the hoary "within the framework of". "Within the purview (scope) of, in the context of, against the background of, in the setting of, as part of, in conjunction with, when . . . is (was) being considered", are a few of the obvious variations. *Dans le cadre du traité* may mean no more than "under the treaty".

Harrap's *Standard French Dictionary* gives a great variety of expressions using the word *cadre*. But only the Supplement, and even that almost as an afterthought, gives the sense in which it is most commonly used nowadays: trained personnel. The term is loosely used and covers a very wide area; and the English equivalent must be chosen with much discrimination according to the context. Some rough equivalents: *Cadres et main d'œuvre*: management and labour; senior officers (officials), élite staff, professional élite, administrative staff (grades), executive staff, executives, managerial staff, "cadres", higher grades, director classes. Strictly, the word should imply supervisory functions, but this is not always the case.

Personnel d'encadrement is sometimes used to translate "supervisory or key staff".

Case (E)

Quiller-Couch, a distinguished forerunner of Fowler and Gowers, carried on a violent campaign against "in the case of". Here is a delightful example of the kind of thing he inveighed against: "In the case of cutlery, the name of a firm in Sheffield was mentioned as one of the leading exporters." (Why not? The cutlery was no doubt made there even if the case wasn't!) "In the case of Japan" probably means no more than "In Japan", and if so it is better said that way.

Cause

Mettre en cause has two somewhat different meanings: (1) involve, incriminate, implicate; (2) question, query, object to. *En connaissance de cause*. Some suggestions for translation: "with full knowledge of the facts, fully informed, with one's eyes open, advisedly, . . . fully considered, with proper awareness . . ., on the basis of a real acquaintance with, properly briefed, in the light of all the factors concerned", etc. *Trancher en connaissance de cause*: to take an informed decision.

Centraliser

"Centralize" is the easy way out. Try "seek a focal point, converge", even "pinpoint" (see *Jargon*) in a particular context.

Certain

Un certain nombre. Often "a number", or merely "some" is better than "a certain number". *Certaines délégations, certains pays*. At times the use of the word "certain" in English gives a nuance not in the original, a suggestion of "without mentioning any names". Note *certains progrès*: "some progress"; *des progrès certains*: "definite progress".

Certes

"Of course, admittedly"; rarely means "certainly".

26

Charge (F)

The large Harrap's Dictionary has an excellent entry under this heading. Note in particular *cahier des charges*: "specifications", etc.; *charges de services des emprunts*: "debt servicing, burden of . . ." etc.

Chargé de

Not "charged with" *But* "responsible for, appointed to, with instructions to, entrusted with, set up to", etc. *Je suis chargé par . . . de*: "I am instructed by . . . to . . .".

Clearly

See *Ambiguity*.

Commas

Translators should avoid the tendency to break up sentences with parentheses, between commas. The effect is often to interrupt the flow of the language unnecessarily. One comma can sometimes be avoided by shifting the parenthetical phrase to the beginning of the sentence, e.g. *Not* "His Government, in all matters relating to shipping, consulted the competent authority" *But* "In all matters relating . . ., his Government consulted . . ." (See *Pseudo-legal language*.)

Comme suit

Often conveniently rendered "this", "these". *Les faits sont comme suit*: "The facts are these:", or simply "The facts are:".

Commun

Le droit commun is *Not* "common law" *But* "ordinary law", sometimes "the law of the land", etc. Common law does not exist in Latin countries. Something similar to it exists in the *droit coutumier* ("customary law") of France and other countries. *Condamné de droit commun*: serving a sentence under criminal law.

Compensateur

Droits compensateurs: countervailing duties.

Compléter

Supplement, amplify, round off, finish off, make up, replenish, add to, bring up to strength. "Complete" is usually translated by French translators as *"achever"*. The inference is plain.

Compromis

Dans un esprit de compromis. Some suggestions: "in a spirit of conciliation (give-and-take), as a concession to, out of deference to (the views of the majority), in an effort to be accommodating, as a conciliatory gesture", etc. Note the legal term *compromis* = an agreement to arbitrate.

Compromettre

"Compromise" as a translation is sometimes ambiguous, sometimes a Gallicism. Try "undermine, jeopardize, challenge", etc., according to the context.

Concret

Suggestions for avoiding "concrete steps": "adopt positive measures, do something practical, make a real effort, give tangible proof".

Condamner

"Condemn" is often too strong. "Denounce" or "censure" or occasionally even "reprove" will get the sense better.

Conditionner

. . . *qui conditionne le développement. Not* "which conditions" *But* "which governs, on which . . . depends". *Conditionnement des denrées*: note the special sense of "packaging".

Conditions

Conditions dans lesquelles. Often "how far . . . to what extent, in what circumstances".

Sous des conditions généreuses. Not "on generous conditions" *But* "on liberal terms".

Préparer la libération prochaine des prisonniers dans d'aussi bonnes conditions que possible. Not "in the best conditions" or "in optimum conditions" *But* "Make adequate preparations for release . . .", or ". . . as efficiently as possible", etc.

. . . *et cela dans les meilleures conditions*: ". . . and is admirably equipped for the purpose".

Congratulate
Note that the preposition in English is "on", not "for". (See *Translatorese.*)

Consacré
In phrases like *un droit consacré dans la Charte*, renderings such as "established, embodied, sanctioned", according to the context, are preferable to "enshrined" (q.v.).

Considérant (noun)
Of a treaty or resolution = preambular paragraph.

Constater
Find, note, conclude, infer, deduce, observe, establish, ascertain, verify, see for oneself, record, certify, state, find facts, place on record, determine, discover, detect, etc.

Contradictoire
The word does ordinarily mean "contradictory", as in English. But in law, *le système judiciaire contradictoire* is the adversary system as opposed to the inquisitorial system. *Une politique non étayée par des preuves contradictoirement discutées*: a policy not supported by evidence argued and counter-argued.

Contrôle
Supervision, inspection, check, verification, control, survey. The meanings of this word in French and of "control" in English have become confused. "Control" in its French sense has now come into official use and cannot be avoided. Where possible, however, one of the other terms mentioned above should be given preference, especially where "control" in the sense of

29

"right of directing" would be open to objection. Cf. also *Lutte contre le paludisme*: malaria control. *Animaux témoins* in experiments: control animals. On the other hand "control" can sometimes be used as a translation of *diriger* (to manage, direct).

Créer

Found, open, establish, institute, form, set up, start, initiate, engender. The word "create" is better confined to phrases where it is normally used in English, e.g. to create an impression or a masterpiece but not a bank or other institution.

Couronné de succès

"Successful" rather than "crowned with success", which is more pompous than the French expression.

D

D'ailleurs

Can sometimes be rendered appropriately by "for that matter".

Dégager

A difficult word to translate when used in conjunction with "principles". Some suggestions: work out, deduce, isolate, discover, discern, ascertain, bring out. *Un principe se dégage . . .*: emerges.

Délicat

Un problème délicat ought to mean an "awkward, tricky", perhaps "sensitive" problem. On the face of it, "knotty, complex" will not do, since the idea of "which needs to be handled with kid gloves" is thus ignored. But "delicate" is not a word to be used readily in this type of context, even assuming that *"délicat"* implies the notion of subtlety in the particular context. The translator should observe carefully whether the writer does not mean simply *"difficile"*, and is merely using the

word *"délicat"* for effect. The context will sometimes make this clear.

Demander (*se*)

M. *se demande si ce n'est pas le cas.* He was inclined to think, thought perhaps that was so, thought that might be so. "Wondered" is not the only way of rendering this word.

Dépouiller

Dépouiller un document, etc. English lacks a good word for the process of extracting the arguments from a speech, the information from a book, etc. This may justify the use of the neologism "to process". "Analyse, scrutinize, collate, make a digest", etc. can also be used in appropriate circumstances.

Dérogation

French would appear to use this word without the slightly "derogatory" nuance attached to the English cognate. "Departure", "exception", at times "waiver" (where renunciation is implied), will give the sense better.

Destiné à

The obvious translation "designed to" is becoming badly overworked in international civil service prose. "Destined to" will seldom do. Try "whose purpose is calculated to, intended for", etc., or simply "for". The English preposition is much stronger than the French.

Développement(s)

Often used in the sense of "passage, discussion, narrative". *Dans les développements qui ont précédé, l'auteur essaie de . . . :* "In the above passage(s) . . .". (See also Part II: *Desarrollar.*)

Dialogue

From time to time a novel term catches the fancy of public speakers and is worked to death for a while, afterwards either disappearing altogether or becoming part of the stock jargon (q.v.) of a particular organization. "Play it by ear" was one such phrase which bedevilled the debates in the United Nations for a long time. I suspect it was popularized by the fact that Dag Hammarskjöld was fond of it. "Dialogue" is a more recent example; it appears to have taken a firm hold and will probably not be dislodged.

Translators who feel reluctant—as they should—to admit such clichés might try whether "discussion, conversation(s), give-and-take, debate (on equal terms)", etc. will not fill the bill equally well or better. "Consensus" is a still more recent example of a term that has "caught on". (See *Jargon*.)

Dictionaries and glossaries

Any translator has a vested interest in knowing what dictionaries, glossaries, terminologies, specialist treatises, etc. are available in the languages he works in. New works of reference are appearing in increasing numbers in all languages. A type of publication of inestimable value to the translator is a bibliography of dictionaries telling him what is available in the various languages on a variety of subjects. Such a volume was published by UNESCO in 1953 under the title of *A Bibliography of Interlingual Scientific and Technical Dictionaries* (1953). Inexplicably, it seems to be unknown to the majority of conference translators. A more recent UNESCO publication: *A Bibliography of Monolingual Technical and Scientific Glossaries (1955-1959)* is also useful. These are of course already somewhat out of date, and it may be that there are other works of reference of the kind published more recently. The compiler of this Handbook would be grateful for particulars of any such valuable material of interest to conference translators.

It is curious that the heading "Dictionaries" in the 1968 edition of the *Encyclopædia Britannica* makes no mention of Harrap's *Standard French Dictionary*, compiled by J. E. Mansion (2 vols.), one of the best bilingual dictionaries in existence.

Difficilement

. . . *peut difficilement voter en faveur* . . . The translation: "It would be difficult for . . . to vote" can be misleading, since there may be no "physical" difficulty whatever, but only a moral one. The word "hardly" in English gives almost exactly the nuance intended, e.g. "His delegation could hardly vote in favour of . . .". In other contexts the translation might be "It would be expecting too much, it would be awkward, embarrassing", ". . . would be reluctant", etc.

Diffuser

"Circulate, disseminate" (information), "propagate" (views), "publicize".

Direction (F)

When the French word means "the heads, those in charge, the people who run something", *direction* is often difficult to translate. We can say "The Office of the Director" if we know there is a director. Frequently we need a vaguer term such as "administration, management, office, department, executive offices", etc. A useful word is Authority: *Direction des Ports et Douane*—Ports and Customs Authority. The word "directorate" is hardly ever used in titles of organizations in English as far as I have observed, except in the BBC, where it appears to be popular; but in the absence of information as to the particular type of *"direction"* in a French text, the translation "directorate" may usefully indicate that the translator is keeping as close to the original as possible.

Directives (E,F)

The English word is much stronger than the French, which is usually better translated as "guidelines, directions, instructions, rules of conduct, broad outline, general lines, guidance," etc.

Discipline (F)

This word occurs constantly in international documentation in the sense of "branch of knowledge, profession", etc. The

33

English cognate with this meaning is something of an archaism, though it seems to be on its way back, and it can be found not infrequently in the "quality" newspapers. "Interdisciplinary" is certainly quite often found in international conference texts, and it may be difficult to avoid both noun and adjective without resorting to a long periphrasis.

Dispositif
"Operative part" of a resolution. *Paragraphe 2 du dispositif*: operative paragraph 2.

Dizaine
See *Non-translation*.

Doctrine, doctrinal (F)
La doctrine often means "the writers on the subject, the orthodox view, orthodoxy, theorists, theory, school of thought", etc.

Double authentique
A true copy.

Dramatic (E), dramatique (F)
We talk nowadays of a landscape or political events as being "dramatic", meaning "sensational". This cliché has seemingly not been taken over as yet by other languages. *Ce qui rend la situation de l'Afrique du Sud encore plus dramatique . . .* might be translated as "What makes the situation . . . still more tragic."

Droit positif
Positive law (i.e. the whole body of legal precepts established or recognized by the State, as opposed to "natural law").

Dynamisme
"Dynamism" in English slightly sets one's teeth on edge, though it is coming to be a common term in economics. "Dynamic force" may be slightly better. A useful neologism

is "drive". Sometimes *dynamisme* means little more than "rapid (vigorous) growth, momentum".

E

Effacement
In addition to the equivalents to be found in the dictionaries, the following may be noted: *En cas d'effacement des fournitures*: "If supplies should run out"; *clause d'effacement*: discontinuance clause.

E.g.
See *Ambiguity*.

Elegant variation
The French language is rather fond of avoiding repetition, e.g. of proper names, by giving a description of the person the second time. Sometimes it is justifiable to ignore this "elegant variation". At other times, even though we are fairly sure the writer's words have been chosen merely to avoid repetition, we are obliged to translate them, since they add something to the meaning of the text: e.g. in the passage ". . . *le livre de M. Gunnar Myrdal. Dans son Introduction, le grand savant suédois . . .*", we can hardly omit to translate *le grand savant suédois*, since the reader may not know who Mr. Myrdal is. "In his Introduction the great Swedish scholar . . .", relating to "Mr. Gunnar Myrdal" in the previous sentence, sounds rather stilted. Instead we could say: "In the Introduction to his book, the eminent Swedish scholar Gunnar Myrdal . . ." (See *Resourcefulness*.)

Elaborer
"Elaborate" will seldom do; "formulate" often sounds pretentious. Say, according to the context, "work out, draw up, sketch, outline, prepare, produce, frame" (q.v.); or in the technical sense "develop, process".

35

Eléments d'appréciation

Not (please!) "elements of appreciation". *But* "criteria, background data, (some) facts, the facts (of the case)", etc.

En effet

"In (point of) fact, indeed", sometimes "actually". Can often be omitted altogether, or the sentence can be combined with the preceding sentence by means of a conjunction such as "for", "since", "because". Since it introduces a clarification, explanation or expansion of what has gone before, a colon will sometimes render *en effet* satisfactorily.

En matière de

Not "in the field of", *But* practically any other conceivable translation, including omission. (See *Field*.)

Enfin

As anyone who has read a fair amount of French must know, this word frequently has no finality about it, but merely means "furthermore, thirdly, fourthly, . . . while, . . . and, again, what is more", etc. and it should be translated accordingly— if it cannot be ignored altogether. *Enfin et surtout.* "Finally and above all" does not ring true. "Last but not least" is sufficiently close to warrant stretching a point in its favour.

Enshrined

A jargon (q.v.) word. *Consacré* (q.v.), which is often translated in this way, is not a sufficiently pompous word to warrant the translation. Say rather "crystallized, which materializes, is embodied, incorporated, contained, present in", etc.

Entreprise

In non-technical documents "undertaking" rather than "enterprise", where it refers to an organization or institution and not to the abstract notion as in "private enterprise". In this sense, French generally uses the word *"initiative"*.

Envisager

"Envisage" is a Gallic-sounding word and a relative upstart in English (early 19th century). "Envision" is a distasteful neologism. "Contemplate, face, consider, anticipate, look forward to, propose, provide for, visualize" (if appropriate), etc. are possible variants.

Etats membres

Logically we should say "Member States" if the expression stands alone, but "States members of . . .". This is the regular practice in the United Nations. But many international organizations have exactly the opposite usage, i.e. "Finland and Sweden are States members"; "The member States of the Organization".

Etc.

There are many useful variants for this abbreviation, e.g. "and so on, and so forth, and the like, and elsewhere, and otherwise, including". *Moyens de paiement tels que les chèques, l'or, etc.*: "cheques, gold or other means of payment", "cheques and gold are some of . . .".

Et cela

Une telle procédure impliquerait l'extension excessive d'une protection conçue pour les individus, et cela en vertu d'un principe non reconnu par tous les Etats. Not "and that", which is poor English (see *Translatorese*) and also ambiguous (see *Ambiguity*). The rather vague force of the construction here might be best rendered by a comma or a dash: ". . . individuals—by virtue of . . .", or if the context will permit, the sentence can be turned and the *"et cela"* eliminated, e.g. "By virtue of a principle . . . such a procedure . . .".

Event

"In the event that": American speakers often use this expression, but it seems to me to have an unfortunate commercialese tang about it. "If" is usually better.

Eventail

L'éventail des salaires, des prix, etc. A favourite word in economic texts. "Range, spread, gamut, spectrum," etc., according to the context.

Eventuellement

If any, if necessary, possibly, perhaps, any . . . that may, such . . . as may, etc. Or omit altogether. "Eventually" is of course a notorious *"faux ami"* of *éventuellement.* (But see Part II: *Eventualmente.*

Exécution

Application, enforcement, execution; sometimes "performance, implementation". *En exécution de*: "in pursuance of".

F

Fâcheux

Vexatious, disconcerting, troublesome, annoying, bothersome, awkward.

Faciliter

The expression "facilitate the solution of a problem" is an ugly example of translatorese (q.v.) *Ces lois prévoient l'accès désormais facilité aux emplois. Not* "These laws provide for facilitating access . . ." *But* ". . . provide for easier access from now onwards (in the future) to . . .". Other words or phrases that can be used are "help, make easier, simplify, make for, . . . for the sake of, in the interests of, make . . . feasible, give opportunities, ease the way for".

Faire la synthèse (de)

Make a conspectus of, piece the facts together, view the matter as a whole, take a syntematic (coherent) view of, bring the facts together, sum up, put in a nutshell.

Faire le point
Sum up, note the trend of, note the stage reached (in the discussion), see where . . . stands, take stock of.

Faire sien
Endorse, sponsor, take over, adopt, identify . . . with.

Field
Extract from a country report on agricultural policy: "In the field of agriculture generally . . .; in the field of citrus and other fruits . . . whereas in the field of dairy products . . .". *Verb. sap.* It seems to me worth while making a real effort to avoid "in the field of" in translation, even though (or perhaps precisely because) it is a handy, all-purpose device. Willingness to take the line of least resistance in this way debases translation and reduces the translator to the level of a hack. There are any number of ways of turning a phrase so as to avoid "field", and almost any alternative is bound to be an improvement, e.g. *activités dans le domaine de la formation et de la recherche*: *Not* "activities in the field of training and research", *But* "training and research activities". Omission of the "field" may be the best translation of all. *Les découvertes en matière des sciences sociales*: *Not* "discoveries in the field of social science" *But* "discoveries in social science".

Fin
A toutes fins utiles: "For such purposes as may be desirable, as thought fit, for (your) attention, for what it is worth, for (information and) any necessary action." Can sometimes be ignored in translation, if it appears to have been used as a meaningless tag to mask a poverty of ideas.

First, firstly
It is no longer regarded as the hall-mark of good English style to write "first, secondly, thirdly". "Firstly" is equally

correct, in spite of De Quincey's condemnation and the fact that some people still feel strongly about it.

Fonction
En fonction de: "As a function of (maths.), (express) in terms of, (vary, move) in sympathy with, according to, (go) hand in hand with."

Etre fonction de: "Be dependent on, proportionate to, vary with (as)." Note that in the United Nations, *commission technique is* "functional committee".

Fonder
See *Baser*.

Forfaitaire
A notoriously difficult word to translate in many contexts. Some suggestions: contract(ual), lump-sum, one-time, blanket, non-recurring, agreed, all-in, outright, flat-rate. *Taxation forfaitaire*: presumptive *or* empirical assessment.

Formel
Not "formal" *But* "categorical, express, strict" (e.g. *il est formellement interdit*).

Formulas, formulae
"The plurals . . . are equally common" (Fowler). There are those who feel that the Latin plural "formulae" should be reserved for mathematics, chemistry, etc.

Formule
Can often be translated simply as "proposal". Other useful words are "device, phraseology, wording, idea, notion, way of putting", or even "principle".

Frame
Beware of the possible *double entendre*: "If the . . . Powers could not frame the resolution, they could at least fix the members of the Committee." (See *Ambiguity*.)

G

Gallicisms

Many of the headings throughout this Handbook are naturally concerned with Gallicisms. The following are examples of constructions that tend to recur frequently and give an unpleasantly Gallic flavour to translation (see also *Translatorese*):

Particulièrement bien placé pour. Not "particularly well placed to" *But* "in a good position to, has an advantage in regard to, unusually apt, specially endowed, competent", etc. (See *Particulièrement.*)

Grâce à. For ways of improving on the obvious rendering see *Thanks to.*

Ce n'est pas parce qu'un traité a pu être signé . . . que les efforts doivent se relâcher. Avoid translating this typically French construction by "It is not because . . . that we can afford . . .", which sounds nonsensical in English. Say "We cannot afford to sit back just because a treaty has been signed," or "The fact that a treaty has been signed does not mean that we can afford to . . .".

Il pourrait accepter de renoncer à ses droits. Not "accept to" *But* "agree to".

. . . est au centre des préoccupations . . . Not "is at the centre of" *But* "is the main concern, is one of the chief worries", etc.

Des efforts remarquables. Not "remarkable efforts" *But* "great, strenuous, considerable efforts".

Translators are prone to become affected by the French tendency to repeat *de* (q.v.) wherever possible, e.g. "Representatives of the Governments of India and of the Republic of South Africa". The logical conclusion here is that each country has more than one Government. (See *Of*, *Translatorese*.)

Deliberate Gallicisms or foreign-sounding phrases such as the following are probably best avoided in translation, since what is intended as sophistication may be mistaken for ignorance: "This notion swears with the facts . . ." *(New Statesman)*.

The new *Modern English Usage* (Fowler/Gowers) has an excellent article under the heading *Gallicisms*. (See also Part II: *Gallicisms*.)

Garanties
Présenter des garanties de sécurité suffisantes. Not "present sufficient guarantees of safety" *But* "conform to the requisite safety standards, offer adequate safeguards . . .".

Global
"Global" is an ugly jargon (q.v.) word, though it is sometimes useful and occasionally unavoidable. Alternatives are "total, aggregate, comprehensive, blanket, over-all (both jargon words), block, all-embracing".

Grammar
A few examples of questionable English grammar taken from translations made in international organizations:

"Il faut conserver le mot 'arbitraire', car en le faisant . . .": "The word 'arbitrary' should *be* retained, since by *doing so* . . ." (by retaining it). The French is perfectly grammatical;

". . . it would not be sufficient to come to an agreement on the *wording* of a test, since the meaning of *those words . . ."* (of the words used);

". . . said that the amount of atomic radiation had *increased* in 1956. To some extent that *increase . . ."* (the increase, i.e., the increase implied. The *word* "increase" has not been used);

"The problem must be *solved,* and he hoped that the plenary session would *do so"* (would solve it);

". . . will not only serve the interests of the German people but also the vital interests of all other States" (will serve not only . . . but also) (see *Both . . . and*);

"We are witnessing changes *initiated* by Governments in the economic and social spheres. They are *doing so* in order to . . ." (The changes are being made *or* They are initiating the changes . . .);

42

"The activities of the High Commissioner's Office were expanding and becoming more and more diversified; the resources at *his* disposal . . ." (at the High Commissioner's disposal—there has been no previous mention of the High Commissioner, only of the Office).

The above insistence on a logical approach to a language as notoriously disdainful of logic as English (see *Style*) may perhaps seem niggling. But at a time when English is being used more and more in international life, it is well for those who have a professional responsibility for the accurate, intelligible, unambiguous and lucid rendering of thought to resist any temptation to slovenliness in the grammatical structure of the language in which they render it.

H

Hand

French is very fond of *d'une part . . . d'autre part*. In English "on the one hand . . . on the other" is best avoided where possible on grounds of style, though it is sometimes difficult to avoid if two subjects joined by "and" are balanced against a third. Sometimes figures: (1) . . . (2) . . . or letters (a) . . . (b) will solve the problem neatly. In a sentence like ". . . encourage peaceful coexistence between the Afro-Asian States on the one hand and Israel on the other" the antithesis is so obvious (even out of context) that, as in boxing, the "hands" can safely be dropped. Other alternatives to the literal rendering are: "which . . . and . . . share with . . .", "contrasting . . . and . . . with . . .", "of . . . and . . . with", ". . . and . . . as compared with . . .", "of the one part . . . of the other part . . ." (in treaties and legal documents), etc.

Harmonie

The vaguely musical suggestion of this word may be less appropriate in English than in the original, and a less colourful word may be more suitable. *En harmonie avec*: "in tune with" is close enough to the metaphor; 'in keeping with, tally with, on the same lines as, in accordance with", etc. *Développement harmonieux*: "smooth development".

Hence
A useful word for rendering various types of construction, e.g. . . . *que les abus sont fréquents: d'où les reproches*: ". . . hence the reproaches."

Historique
Past (previous) history, historical background, genesis, antecedents, chronological account, (past) record, (historical) retrospect, survey, previous events, background facts, what has (already) happened (taken place, been done) in a matter.

Huit jours, quinze jours
The curious way of counting the beginning and ending dates in a week or a fortnight, a common feature of many languages, raises an awkward problem in translation. In England a sentence of *"huit jours au violon"* would be "Seven (not eight) days in clink", and in a non-technical sense *huit jours, quinze jours* is best rendered as "a week, a fortnight". Legally, however, these terms tend to be interpreted literally, especially where this will give the benefit of the doubt to the person concerned. Thus in French legal procedure, a time-limit or a grace period of *"huit jours"* of which notification was given on Monday morning at 0001 hrs. will expire on Tuesday at midnight the following week. On the other hand, a person sent to prison for *"huit jours"* on the same day at 11.59 p.m. will be released on the following Tuesday (in practice at noon). English legal texts sometimes use the expression "seven clear days, fourteen clear days". In case of doubt, it is safer to translate literally "eight, fifteen".

Humanité
This word has to do for the abstract notion of "humanity" and also for the more tangible notion of "people" for which English has the excellent word "mankind". Other alternatives when the word is used in this more usual sense are "people(s)

44

of the world, people everywhere, man, men, the human race",
etc. (See *Peoples*.)

Idioms

Colourful language adds to the readability of almost any
reading matter, as we discover from reading articles on Mid-
Western politics given a somewhat bogus fascination by *Time
Magazine*'s reporters. International conference prose can be
devastatingly drab. But two dangers must be guarded against
in any attempt to brighten it up. The first is making the
translation decidedly more colourful than the original and thus
misrepresenting it and perhaps giving it a superficial glitter
which the author may resent; the other, even more important,
is using language which will not be understood by readers
whose understanding of English may be not very profound.
Even an innocent expression like: "The allegation proved to
be mistaken", used by a United Nations English-speaking
representative, provoked a retort that no proof had ever been
submitted!

The conference translator should resist the temptation to
introduce idioms if they are not likely to be understood by
persons whose mother-tongue is not English. He may perhaps
be justified if he is translating an idiom he himself has to look
up!

Illusoire

Mythical, a bubble, unrealistic, an illusion, deceptive, sham,
bogus, a snare and a delusion. "Illusory" has a slightly Gallic
tinge.

Imagination

Perhaps the main purpose of this Handbook is to try to bring
home to translators the danger of falling into a dull routine
and the need for keeping the mind fresh and alert. Staleness

is an occupational disease of the translator and the best way to combat it is to use the imagination. Here are one or two examples of unimaginative translation:

'*Aux Etats-Unis . . .; dans ce même pays.*' "In the U.S.A. . . . that same country" (no English-speaking person would dream of saying that). *Say* "likewise (again, also) in the United States . . .". (See *Elegant variation.*)

. . . *Le Secrétaire-Général, dont les devoirs multiples et urgents sont bien connus de tous.* Means no more than "as everyone knows, he has a thousand urgent things to think of . . ." (but see *Paraphrasing*).

"In some of the United States" reads oddly. "In some states of the United States" is little better. The translator should try to manipulate the sentence, e.g. "In the United States, there are some states which . . .".

. . . *tend à renforcer la protection nécessaire de l'administration contre les critiques . . .* Not "is designed to strengthen the necessary protection of the administration against the criticism . . ." *But* "to reinforce the protection which must be given to . . . in the face of . . .".

Le Secrétaire-Général doit être félicité des efforts qu'il a accomplis et dont il a donné un aperçu dans son rapport Not ". . . on the action he has taken, of which an account is given . . ." *But* "on the action he has taken, as outlined in . . .".

. . . *devraient faire l'effort nécessaire pour . . .* Not "make the necessary effort to . . ." *But* "make the effort (*or* whatever effort was) needed to . . .".

. . . *depuis douze ans; certes, on n'est pas resté inactif durant cette longue période* Not "throughout that long period" *But* "for all that (length of) time";

'*Un problème unique dans l'histoire du monde* Not "in the history of the world" *But* "in history".

Voilà le grandiose aspect positif Not "This is the grandiose positive aspect" *But* "This is the positive (q.v.) outlook, and an impressive one it is".

(See also *Resourcefulness, Translatorese.*)

Impersonal construction

Literal translation or unimaginative précis-writing will produce poor English like the following: "It is precisely in order to do so-and-so that it is important to . . ."; "It was clear that it was the implementation of that provision which the refugees desired above all else" (Why not "that the implementation . . . was what the refugees desired . . ."?); "If it was desired to maintain the principle of unanimity, it was necessary to act through persuasion". (Why not "If the principle . . . was to be maintained, the (Committee etc.) must use . . ."?). No self-respecting translator or précis-writer should pass such English. Ways of avoiding "It was necessary to" at the beginning of sentences in translating passages in reported speech:
1. Turn the sentence into the passive, with "should, had to be", etc.
2. "There had to be, ought to be, was a need for"
3. ". . . meant doing, insisting", etc.
4. "What was needed was . . ."
5. ". . . was the answer to the problem of . . ."

On voit que. Not "One sees that" *But* "It is evident (clear) that."

Important (F)

Often = "large, extensive, sizable, substantial", especially when referring to money, costs, savings, e.g., *des sommes importantes.*

Inconvénient

Not as a rule "inconvenience" *But* "drawback, snag, disadvantage, awkward situation", etc.

Indirect speech

An important aspect of conference translation is producing an English version of précis or minutes of meetings written up in other languages, first and foremost French. In French, of course, "summary records" are written in the present tense, and have to be turned into past-tense *oratio obliqua* in the translation. The proper sequence of tenses is ordinarily very straightforward: *il pense* = "he thought" or "was thinking"; *il pensait* = "he had thought" or "had been thinking". But the automatic change of tenses, and of "this" to "that", "now" to "then", etc., can result in ponderous and even ambiguous English, e.g. "When I was young and read the newspaper, I always felt . . ." To say "When he had been young and had read the newspaper he had always felt . . ." is both absurd and misleading. "When he was young and read the newspaper, he had always felt . . ." is clearer and reads better. A single pluperfect is often sufficient to draw together a series of past tenses.

Another difficulty in translating reported speech is that expressions like "as regards" sound wrong when all the verbs are in the past, yet do not readily lend themselves to change— "as regarded" or "that was to say" sound even worse. It is better to write "with (in) regard to, as to", etc. Again, expressions like "at this stage" should not automatically be rendered as "at that stage" unless it is clear what stage, or what moment of time, is referred to. Words like "ago", "now" can often be left, e.g. "He said he would now discuss . . ."; "two months ago there had been . . ." Literal application of the rules is carrying logic too far; we must take advantage of the "graphic" facilities of English.

Insister

"*Insister sur*" frequently does *Not* mean "insist on", which is much stronger and more categorical. "Press for, urge, dwell on, call attention to". *Je ne veux pas insister*: I do not wish to labour the point.

Inspiré

Les motifs qui ont inspiré . . . The word "inspired" still retains some trace of its godlike origin, and is best kept for very special occasions. In French it has become debased. ". . . underlying, actuating" would suffice. "Based on, derived from, . . . took the idea from, activated by", etc. could also be used in certain contexts. (See *Baser*.)

Inter alia

Although it is impossible to avoid using this unpleasing tag occasionally, other turns of phrase should be tried: e.g., *"Le régime s'est servi, entre autres, de la . . ." ". . .* has used such devices as . . ."; "Methods used by . . . have included . . ." Remember that *alia* is a Latin neuter plural, and therefore the expression cannot refer to persons. "Including" is sometimes all that is needed, or "partly" can be worked in.

Intercalaire

Intérêts intercalaires: Interest payable while work is in progress.

Intéressant

Often "important, valuable, profitable, advantageous, attractive, promising, intriguing," rather than "interesting".

Intéressé (l')

"The person concerned" is preferable in some contexts to "the interested party" which may sound slightly pejorative.

Intermédiaire

Par l'intermédiaire de: "Through the intermediary of" is a Gallicism. "Through, through the medium (agency) of, via, using the good offices of", etc.

Interrogative sentences

Good English translators seem instinctively to shun direct questions (generally rhetorical) introduced into a text and then answered. It is usually an easy matter, especially in reported speech, to get round the difficulty, e.g. *"N'est-il pas évident que . . .?"* "Surely it was evident . . ." There seems to be something slightly naive about the direct question device, though it must be admitted that many sophisticated languages make liberal use of it.

49

Intervenir

Take a hand, mediate, take action, act in the matter, make a *démarche*, make an approach, act as go-between, make a statement, speak, hold forth, have one's say. "Intervention" in English may give a suggestion that some kind of trouble has arisen, e.g. "Government intervention in the wage dispute". *Intervention* in French is of course regularly used in the sense of "speech, statement" and just occasionally "intervention" may be a suitable translation in English, where neither "statement" nor "speech" would be appropriate.

Inverted commas

For the reason given under *"Brackets"* (q.v.), translators should be familiar with the normal rules for the position of inverted commas enclosing quotations. The principle is in fact similar to that applied to parenthetical matter. The following examples illustrate the general rule:—
1. The resolution reads: "This shall be done."
2. The resolution states that "this shall be done".

In other words, when the phrase or sentence is a complete entity, the quotation marks come after the full stop; when the words quoted form part of the sentence, they are first "unquoted" and then comes the full stop to end the sentence. A notable exception to this is the practice followed by some publishers where a longish quotation ending a paragraph forms part of the sentence and therefore should end: "unquote, full-stop". To give the text a rounded-off appearance the "full-stop, unquote" order is followed. Translators can safely follow the above general rules.

J

Jargon

The loyalties of the English translator must include a large measure of loyalty to the English language. One of the difficulties of translating for international organizations where the spoken word plays an important role is that such organizations tend to develop a special jargon of their own which does not necessarily enrich the mainstream of the language. Two factors in particular encourage the formation of the jargon sometimes referred to as "delegatese". The first is the fact that much of the spoken and written material to be found in conference documents is produced by people whose mother-tongue is not that in which they are writing or speaking. The second factor is the influence of the interpreter's style on the form of speech used by speakers at conferences. It is no reflection on the competence of conference interpreters to say that the very speed with which they work leaves them no time for weighing their words, so that they tend to follow the original language closely. Thus expressions like "seized of", "intervention" (q.v.), "within the framework of", "item inscribed in the agenda", are heard constantly and even printed in the records of conference deliberations. As a result they gradually gain a spurious currency among English speakers. The translator has more time than the interpreter to weigh the kind of language he uses. Hence without being over-literary or academic, he should endeavour to resist the inroads of the convenient cliché, pompous pseudo-scientific phraseology, etc., of which the following are good examples:

"The survey and identification of primary principles had developed into a recognition of the widest requirements and conditioning factors for successful practice through supporting measures in all related parts." (Whatever does it mean?)

Quotation from a speech: "I find it hard to make out what is meant by integrating the activities of agencies into services and objectives." (So do I!):

. . . *le délai permettrait aux partis d'assurer le rapatriement.* ' *Not* "the prescribed period would enable the parties to ensure repatriation" *But* "the intervening period would allow time for the parties to arrange for the repatriation". (See also *Assurer, Faciliter, Dialogue, Level, Negative.*)

Job

There was a time when United Nations translation practice

proscribed this word in the sense of "employment, work, situation". But "job-workers", "employment by the job", have long been official ILO terms, and the word has probably acquired sufficient respectability to warrant its general use. In a phrase like *"Un projet destiné à créer deux mille nouveaux emplois . . . '* it is difficult to avoid calling them "jobs". "Posts" is too grand and "work for 2,000 people" does not mean quite the same thing.

L

Lacune
Combler une lacune need not always be "fill a gap". "Make good a deficiency, rectify an omission", or some such variant may suit the context better.

Last
See *Ambiguity*. "At the last meeting". (Previous? or final?)

Lecture
Le président donne lecture: Not "read" *But* "read out"; otherwise it may seem to imply "read quietly to himself, and didn't tell a soul".

Legal language
Personne ne doit: In legal texts *Not* "No one may" *But* "No person shall". The United Kingdom Statutes are recommended as background reading for translators of legal texts.

Lengthy
Some people object to this word on the grounds that "long" is better. But the two words are clearly not altogether synonymous.

Level
Another jargon word—"inquiry on the national level". If it is unavoidable, let us at least say "at the national level". The

idea can sometimes be expressed differently, e.g. "inquiry carried out throughout the country, nationally; nation-wide inquiry", etc. "Arranged at the level of . . ." may well mean simply "arranged by".

Light, lines
"In the light of", "on (along) the lines of". Useful phrases—but should not be overdone. Some translators and editors rule them out completely.

Limitatif
See *Restrictif*.

Loi
This is better translated as "Act" rather than "Law" when referring to a specific piece of legislation. Note *projet de loi* "draft legislation", "bill"; *décret-loi*, "legislative decree". (Since this was written, the United Nations has placed the stamp of approval on "decree-law".)

Lutte(r)
La lutte contre (a disease, etc.) is best turned by the use of "campaign, control, action (to put down), preventive measures", etc. Cf. Anti-(malaria) campaign.

M

Magistrat
Not "magistrate" *(juge d'instruction)* But "judge", or more generally "law officer".

Maîtrise
In conference work, "supervisory staff, superintendence" or "expertise, mastery" is likely to be the meaning of this term, which can signify a variety of things.

Mandat

Terms of reference, mandate, powers, authority, commission, mission. *Sans mandat*: unauthorized. *Sans mandat judiciaire*: without a warrant issued by the court.

Manifestation

"Demonstration, event, celebration, show", rather than "manifestation", if the idea of "parade" is intended.

Méthodologie

This word is often used loosely to mean nothing more than "method(s)", "system", etc. and should be so translated unless it clearly means "methodology", which is a much broader concept.

Mettre au point

Revise, review, edit, put the finishing touches to, rectify, polish, put into final form, develop (of a system). In technical texts "adjust, tune".

Ministère public

It is better not to translate this term, since it has no real equivalent in English. But a rough equivalent (e.g. "Cf. the Public Prosecutor") in the form of a footnote may be useful to the reader. It is of course arguable that this is shirking the responsibility of the translator to render everything in the original. The difficulty here is that "State Counsel's Office" does not really give a true picture. Strangely enough, the term *Ministère public* is used for the actual person representing the Government before the court. (See also *Non-translation*.)

Ministre, ministère

Be careful to distinguish between the two. It is easy to misread them when both words occur more than once in a short passage. But see *Ministère public* above.

Motion d'ordre

Point of order. *Motion* is strictly a "procedural motion",

though it is often used loosely to mean simply "proposal".

Motivé

When used with *avis, sentence,* etc.: "with statement of reasons, reasoned, supported by evidence, giving the grounds for". In non-technical texts "justified, warranted, motivated by, sound".

Multiple (F)

This word is used far more frequently in French than "multiple" in English. "(The) many, numerous, many and varied, scores of, a variety of, multitudinous, many instances of, vast numbers of, whole series of", etc.

N

National (F)

Promouvoir une spécialisation nationale adéquate. Not "national specialization" *But* "specialization in the country" (or "in various individual countries").

Negative (E)

The French, Spanish, Russian and other equivalents of this word have come to be used as a kind of *omnium gatherum*, useful to speakers who cannot or do not wish to find a more precise adjective, e.g. "Tito described the U2 affair as a negative event" *(The New York Times)*. What he presumably meant was "an event which puts the clock back, which does harm, is retrograde, is retrogressive". Translators should combat this vague use of the word. *Prédictions négatives. Not* "negative predictions" *But* "pessimistic forecasts, prophecies of doom", etc. Other possible equivalents: adverse, unhelpful, unforthcoming, reactionary, unpromising, unproductive, obstructive, obstructionist, step in the wrong direction, defeats the purpose. (See also *Positive, Jargon.*)

Niveau

Niveau de vie. Demographers call this "level(s) of living", i.e. the actual conditions, as opposed to *standard de vie*: "standard of living", i.e. the conditions regarded as fitting and proper in a given context. "Norm" is also used technically as meaning "desirable conditions as defined for specific purposes". It must be confessed that population specialists do not appear to abide very strictly by their own definitions.

Nom

Au nom de. Generally speaking, "on behalf of" is preferable to "in the name of".

Nommer

Not as a rule "nominate" (*désigner*) *But* "appoint".

None

Gowers' view (*ABC of Plain Words*) may be worth recalling: "*None* may be used indifferently with a singular or plural verb. The plural used to be commoner, but the singular has been catching up recently, probably under the mistaken impression that it is more correct because it is more logical." Among the conference translator fraternity, I have yet to meet anyone who was not distinctly in favour of the singular.

Non-translation

The question whether titles of organizations or books, and words like *Ministère public*, or in other languages *caboclo, Autobahn* or *junta* which have no ready equivalent should be translated, is a constant source of perplexity in translating. Where the sponsoring organization does not lay down hard-and-fast rules, the question the translator must ask himself is: "Does translation provide useful information for a reader who does not understand the original language?" For example, the name and address of a firm sending a letter must obviously be left in the original, in a form which can be copied as it stands by anyone who wishes to reply to the letter. The title of a book would not ordinarily be translated, since without an explanation an English version might suggest that a translation exists. On the other hand, an indication of the title in brackets after the original, e.g. "(Translation of title: The Public Services in the Developing Countries)" might be of such interest to the reader that he would wish to have the book even if he had to have it specially translated. The United Nations practice in regard to the translation of names of institutions is not to translate them if they are commonly referred to under their original titles, e.g. *Riksdag, Bundestag, Dáil,* etc. But a literal translation is added where it seems likely to be of use to the reader. Inevitably, the decision must ordinarily be left to the translator.

As a general rule, foreign currencies, measurements, etc. must obviously be left as they stand, e.g. hectares need not be converted into acres, or kilometres into miles. But where the reference is to mere "distance" and not to "distance as measured in countries using the metric system", it would be legitimate and sensible to translate . . . *ports à des milliers de kilomètres de distance* as "harbours thousands of miles away". A phrase like *"quelques dizaines de cas"* may involve an inspired guess as to the probable number intended, e.g. "a score or more, a score or two, twenty or thirty, a few dozen", etc.

The corollary to non-translation, namely the insertion of things not in the original, is likewise a matter of discretion. Resolutions, legal texts, etc. must obviously be treated with the utmost respect. But in run-of-the-mill conference documents, it may be wise to clarify by a judicious addition, e.g. In a document citing many numbers, figures, etc. which at one point says "(voir chiffre III/9)" it is clearly wise to specify "see III/9 below" or "article III, para. 9 of the treaty" etc. even if this is not in the text.

Norme

In addition to "norm" and "standard", there are many words which can be used to advantage, according to the context, to translate *norme,* e.g. rule, regulation, code, yardstick, benchmark, pattern, criterion, mould, policy. *Normatif* is often used in the sense of "law-making, policy-making, standard-setting".

Notamment

As often as not, the best way to translate this word is to ignore it. "Particularly, notably" are in most contexts too strong; "for example, for instance, among others, such as, including, *inter alia*" (q.v.) may give the sense better, if it has any force at all. As often as not, it is used as a device for achieving sentence rhythm, and can be ignored.

Note verbale

A form of third-person diplomatic communication, usually between Governments. In United Nations practice, the term is left untranslated and not underlined.

Nuance

One of the great joys of language study, and one of the most valuable assets of the translator, is a subtle appreciation of fine shades of meaning. The English language is second to none in its wealth of nuance. Examples are to be found *passim* in this Handbook (see *Aspirations*, *Lengthy*, *Relative Clauses*, etc.).

O

Objectif

"Objective" in English suggests either photography or pomposity (q.v.). "Purpose, aim(s), object, target, goal" are all good alternatives.

Of

In the French phrase *"priveraient l'Organisation de son expérience et de la contribution que . . ."* the second *de* is indispensable. English frequently dispenses with the "of" on stylistic grounds, unless it is needed to avoid ambiguity: ". . . would deprive the country of his experience and the contribution he had made . . ." is perfectly clear without the *de*. In the sentence "Half the staff members recruited during the past five years were nationals of the United States and its Western military allies", it might be argued that without an "of" before "its", the sentence *could* mean that half the staff *were* the allies of the United States. But, except in legal and similar texts, English tends to rely on the context rather than on logical fool-proof construction, which makes for ponderous, foreign-sounding prose. (See *Gallicisms, Ambiguity.*)

Only

Fowler/Gowers' *Modern English Usage* has a very interesting article on the position of "only" in the sentence. The summing-up is worth quoting: "There is an orthodox position for the adverb, easily determined in case of need; to choose another position that may spoil or obscure the meaning is bad; but a change of position that has no such effect except technically is both justified by historical and colloquial usage and often demanded by rhetorical needs." A corollary for the conference translator may be helpful. Many of Fowler's examples of deliberately misplaced "only" are obviously spoken forms and are to be read with the speech intonation in mind. Since the conference translator's raw material tends perhaps more often than not to be "prose for speaking", he must take care that what seems perfectly clear to him, with the original in mind or indeed in front of him, will be equally clear to the reader approaching it as "literature". In case of doubt, it is surely better to be clear than to be "heterodox", to use Fowler's term.

"Seulement" or *"ne . . . que"* is often effectively translated by "not . . . unless", "not . . . except when", "not . . . until" rather than "only".

Opposer

A curious use of this word may serve as a warning to the translator not to accept a term that makes nonsense in a particular context without checking whether it can have an entirely different meaning. The sentence *C'est une règle d'ordre public pouvant être opposée en tout état de cause,* if translated

59

as "a rule that can be challenged", would mean the opposite of what the writer obviously intended. If we recall that when in the United Nations Security Council *"L'Union Soviétique oppose son veto"* it is hardly likely to be challenging its own veto but exercising it, we may be prompted to look up the word in Harrap. *Opposer une exception*: raise an objection, demur (in law) may give us the clue. In the first instance above, *"invoquée"* would be better French, or at least less likely to be misunderstood. (For a similar case in Spanish, see Part II: *Cancelar*.)

Ordonnance, ordre

For the sake of uniformity, *ordonnance* is perhaps best translated as "ordinance", *ordre* or *arrêté* as "order".

Ordre

Dans cet ordre d'idées: "In that connection, from that angle, while on the subject."

Orientation (F)

Directing, direction, convergence, aim, concentration, planning, policy, steering, "beaming" (line of) approach, trend, bias, guidance; sometimes "views"; "orientation" is only occasionally a satisfactory translation.

Ouvrage d'art

Not "work of art" (*œuvre d'art*) *But* "engineering project (works), bridge, tunnel, structure, overpass, underpass", etc., according to context. In railway terminology the plural form can often be rendered "bridges and/or tunnels, etc.". "Structure" is perhaps the most acceptable blanket term, and the one most frequently used in technical literature.

P

Paragraphing

The division of a text into paragraphs has a definite purpose. The paragraph combines sentences dealing with the same subject-matter, making the passage more readable, simplifying the task of reference, and giving the text a well-ordered look.

Writers frequently disregard this function of the paragraph entirely. There is a strong tendency, especially in documents intended to be read aloud, to make every sentence a paragraph. The translator is not compelled to respect this practice, unless it is clear that the translation will be used for comparative purposes and that therefore the two texts should *look* alike.

Paraphrasing

Translators should beware of the temptation to re-write sentences so as to give the general sense while expressing the thought differently, even though more neatly. There is no doubt an element of editing in all translation, but the translator must remember that good translation attempts to approximate to the form as well as the content of the original text.

Generally speaking, the particular emphasis which the order of the parts of a sentence in French (and indeed in most Western languages) produces is not likely to be appreciably upset if they are translated in the same order as in the original text. The order may have to be changed, if only because different languages have different devices for expressing emphasis; but there is no virtue, and not a little risk, in arbitrarily changing the sequence of the parts of the original sentence. For the conference translator there is a further and very significant reason for keeping the original order wherever possible. Documents are frequently discussed sentence by sentence, each person using the text in his own language. It may be impossible to locate a phrase or passage if it has been turned upside down in the translation.

Parquet

This word when used in the legal sense should be left untranslated. (See *Non-translation*.) If necessary, a footnote can be added: "Nearest English equivalent = Public Prosecutor's Office."

Part

D'autre part rarely means "on the other hand" *(au contraire* or *par contre)*. Usually it means "moreover", or "further". It can frequently be omitted as one of the linking devices which French favours more than English. "For (its) part" is a useful means of giving in a written text the emphasis which would be given by a stress accent or intonation in speech; but if it can be avoided by rearrangement of the words, so much the better, e.g. *Not* "For its part, the Australian delegation felt . . ." *But* "The Australian delegation did feel, however . . ." *or* "What the Australian delegation felt, however, was that . . .". (See also *Hand*.)

Particulièrement

To translate this word as "particularly" may at times introduce a nuance not in the original. In French the word is often used without any comparative implication, whereas in English it suggests "more than in other cases or circumstances". "Very, extremely, unusually" may be better. *Les provisions étaient particulièrement maigres*: "The provisions were of the scantiest." (See *Gallicisms*.)

Party

Party *to* a convention, Contracting Parties *to*, not *of*.

Peoples

To translate *"les peuples"* by "the peoples" without other qualification is somehow unsatisfactory. Alternatives: "people generally, the nations of the world, people everywhere, the masses throughout the world, all peoples, the population of the world, the inhabitants of the earth", etc. (Cf. "All people that on earth do dwell".) One or other of the above may suit a particular context. "A people" is a singular noun; but when "the people" is used it is often a matter of judgement whether the verb should be singular or plural. (See also *Populations*.)

Per capita

Fowler (*Modern English Usage*) denounces *per capita* as being incorrectly used. I do not find his argument convincing; indeed it is hard to see the logic of *"per caput"* as meaning "per" head, since *per*=each ("per tuppence per pound") is hardly Latin, whereas *per capita*(=by, through heads) makes sense. Be that as it may, Fowler was too enlightened a scholar and too sensitive a linguist not to realize that to apply logic to the development of English usage is a losing battle. Even in his day, *per capita* was probably already too securely rooted to be dislodged; nor do I believe that he intended that *per caput* should actually replace *per capita*, even though he called the latter "a modern blunder". Certainly he would have thought differently forty years after he wrote his article, and it is disappointing to find that the new edition by Gowers does not bring Fowler up to date on this point.

Permanent

International jargon has adopted the useful word "continuing" for expressions like *"des arrangements permanents"*, where something less than perpetuity is envisaged. Cf. also *comité permanent*: standing committee.

Permettre

Une attitude pareille permettrait d'atteindre . . . I should like to put in a plea for more general use of the verb "make for" in this type of phrase.

Personne

The usual translation of *personne physique, personne morale* is "individual, corporation (corporate body, body corporate, legal entity")", etc. In a context where it is desirable to balance the two terms, "physical person" and "juridical (artificial) person" may be found useful.

Plénier

En séance plénière: "in (the) plenary meeting" rather than "in plenary", which is rather colloquial.

Plus ou moins

In English "more or less" is a more closely knit expression than the Romance equivalent, and usually means "relatively, fairly". It can of course have the same meaning in Latin languages too; but a phrase like . . . *à des intervalles plus ou moins longs* could equally well be written . . . *à des intervalles qui peuvent être longs ou courts*, i.e. at varying intervals. Sometimes it may be desirable to paraphrase to get the sense: *dans un langage plus ou moins clair*: "in language which may be clear or may not", "which is not always (necessarily) clear".

Plusieurs

There seems to be a growing tendency to translate this word as "many" rather than "several, quite a few". *Un ou plusieurs*: "one or more".

Pomposity

Words like *formuler, élaborer*, which are perfectly ordinary in a Latin language, may sound pompous in their English equivalents. The Anglo-Saxon word will often be a more satisfactory equivalent precisely because it is the everyday word. (See *Elaborer*.)

Population(s)

To translate *"les populations"* as "the populations" without qualification is even less satisfactory than to translate *les peuples* as "the peoples". "The populations of (the countries referred to)", "people", etc. (See *Peoples*.)

Position

Mais il est difficile d'expliquer la position d'une délégation qui . . . rejette maintenant. As an alternative to "position" try "attitude, outlook, stand taken, reasoning, way of thinking", etc. "Rationale" is a popular jargon word.

Positive (E)

It is sometimes desirable in translation to "interpret" according to the context the peculiar force or colour of these vague "blanket" words like *"positif, négatif"* (see *Negative)* or their equivalent in other languages (Eastern-bloc terminology is especially fond of them). Suggestions: progressive (q.v.), practical, forthcoming, helpful, successful, forward-looking, productive, in the right direction, optimistic, real, genuine, constructive, encouraging, favourable. (See also *Droit positif.)*

Préciser

Define, specify, state precisely (exactly), define more accurately, go (further) into detail, make clear, say for certain, give in detail, furnish full particulars of, state (categorically, explicitly). It often means no more than "state, explain" or even "say". (See *Souligner.)*

Présence

Not as a rule "presence" *But* "The fact that there is, the existence of" (see *Absence).* Phrases like "a United Nations presence in the Middle East" are common currency in the press nowadays, and must no doubt be reluctantly accepted.

Président, présidence

It is hardly necessary to remind translators that *président* may be either "President" or "Chairman". *La présidence*: The Chair, the office of president, the presiding officers. Sometimes used instead of *"le Bureau"* to mean "the officers".

Préventif

Détention préventive. Not "preventive detention" *But* "remand in custody" (while awaiting trial). "Preventive detention" is used for persistent offenders. In French it is often rendered as *internement administratif.*

Premier

Pendant les premières années de l'après-guerre. Not "During (In) the first post-war years" *But* ". . . the early (earlier) . . .".

Problem

A League of Nations reviser apparently on one occasion counted an average of nine "problems" per page in a document of ninety pages. The author said he knew of no alternative word! *Problème* is often better translated by a less weighty word—"question, matter, issue, subject, topic, point, difficulty, obstacle", etc.

Procureur

Le Procureur de la République is not the same as the Public Prosecutor or the Attorney-General. The term should therefore be left untranslated (see *Non-translation*); if a translation is unavoidable, "Chief State Counsel" is perhaps the least unsatisfactory. In court, the *Procureur* acts rather in the same way as the Counsel for the Crown in England.

Progressif

"Progressive" is a dangerous word, since it may suggest "advanced, left-wing" (*progressiste*) when the meaning is "gradual, steady, one after another", etc. The translator should make sure that no such nuance can be read into the text if he uses the word.

Projet

Note that the annual *Projet de budget* of the United Nations is called "Budget estimates" in English. Other international organizations distinguish between *projet de budget* = draft budget, and *prévisions budgétaires* = budget estimates.

Proposal

This word should be generally avoided in translating the records of meetings and elsewhere if the terms "draft resolution" or "resolution" can be correctly used instead.

Proposer (F)

Il propose de créer un fonds: "He proposed the creation of a fund" or "that a fund should be set up", *Not* "He proposed to create a fund" (unless he was intending to do it himself, in which case the French would be *il se propose*. (But see *Créer*.)

Propriété

More usually "ownership" than "property". *Une propriété*: "an estate".

Pseudo-legal language

Translators seem at times to wish to give an important look to non-technical texts by inserting subordinate clauses, between commas, in the middle of their sentences, e.g. "All the secondary schools in the Territory have, for classes which started after September 1958, adopted the Belgian curriculum." (Why not put the parenthetical phrase either at the beginning of the sentence or at the end, according to the emphasis required?) *L'Office devrait, en collaboration avec les gouvernements* . . . (Why not: "In collaboration with . . ., the Agency should . . ."?) In a sentence like "The court may, in cases which do not involve certain serious crimes, impose a fine", the parenthesis may be justifiable, on the grounds that the sentence is a paraphrase of a legal provision. But as a general rule this "Civil Service prose" should be used with discrimination. In general it may be said that legal English is entirely appropriate in a legal text, but is out of place as ordinary English prose. (See also *Commas*.)

Punctuation

The original punctuation of a document need not necessarily be followed slavishly in the translation. French writers in particular often use a comma where English would use a semi-colon, and a semi-colon where English would favour a full stop.

The sentence need not be regarded as an unassailable, sacrosanct unit. Whereas in translating German, the sentence has constantly to be split up if it is to make readable English, in the Latin languages sentences can frequently be strung together. (See also *Paragraphing*.)

67

Q

Qualité
Of a judge (magistrate) *Not* "status" *But* "competence".

Quinze jours
See *Huit*.

R

Rappeler
French précis-writers use this word as a stock means of achieving variety in introducing speakers' remarks, without any suggestion of "calling back to mind", or "recollecting". Hence to translate it automatically as "recall" may distort the speaker's intention.

Réduit
Just as *adapté à* (q.v.) has lost the verbal force which "adapted to" still seems to retain, so with *réduit* and "reduced". If *"malgré le temps réduit dont le Conseil dispose"* is translated as ". . . the reduced time . . ." there is a suggestion that the Council previously had more time but it has now been curtailed. "Limited time" is much more recognizably an *expression toute faite* meaning "shortness of time". But why not simply use an abstract noun in such cases? e.g. *Les problèmes sérieux . . . justifient cette attitude.* The translator should ask himself whether the context does not call for "The seriousness (gravity) of the problems justifies this".

Référer
Il n'y a pas d'objection à ce que le texte se réfère à la résolution. If we say "should refer to" it could mean either *"have* reference to" or *"make* reference to". If we know from the context which is meant, the translator should make it clear. (See *Ambiguity*.)

Relative clauses

French very often uses what appears to be a strict relative clause when there is a distinct causal implication. Translators should not blindly render the original literally, e.g. *Mon pays, qui n'a jamais souffert du colonialisme, s'honore pourtant . . . Not* ". . . which has never . . . is nevertheless . . ." *But* ". . . although it has never . . . is . . .";

La délégation française, qui participe depuis douze ans aux travaux, estime . . . To reproduce something of the vaguely causal nuance, we might say ". . . after taking part (*or* having taken part) . . . considered";

Il remercie les représentants de la Pologne et de la République Arabe Unie qui ont contribué . . . Not "who had contributed" *But* "for their contribution";

Tout esprit objectif ne peut en imputer la responsabilité qu'à la partialité du Secrétaire-Général et de ses collaborateurs immédiats, qui cherchent à favoriser les pays occidentaux. Not "who sought to favour" *But* "and their desire to" (i.e., it is not a general statement of their wishes; the *"qui cherchent . . ."* explains the *"partialité"*).

In contradistinction to the above examples, French also at times seems to use a subordinate clause for stylistic reasons when there is no subordination of the idea contained in the clause, e.g. *"L'usine, qui a un personnel de 600 hommes, comprend deux ateliers . . ."* In the context it is clear that the writer is merely giving a description of the various facilities of the plant. To translate this as "The plant, which has a staff of 600, consists of . . ." gives a slight idea of subordination to the parenthetical phrase, as if this information were of lesser importance. It would be better in English to make two separate sentences: "The plant has a staff of 600. There are two workshops, etc."

Reprendre

Le paragraphe reprend les dispositions de l'Article . . . de la Charte: "the paragraph reproduces the terms of Article . . . of the Charter". *Reprendre une suggestion*: "repeat" (sometimes "revive, resubmit, restate, adopt, take up", even "borrow", according to the context). The "re" does not necessarily have the force of repetition or iteration.

Répression

(Prevention and) punishment, repression. "Suppression", though it is found in a number of conventions, is not a real equivalent. It is rather the completion of the process of *répression*.

Réserver

Depuis quelques semaines, l'actualité internationale réserve à la crise du Congo ses commentaires les plus sensationnels. Not ". . . news reports have reserved their most . . ." *But* "have devoted . . . to", etc. In other contexts "concentrate on, expend on, lavish on", etc. *Il se réserve de soutenir la question plus tard. Not* "reserved the right to", *But* "proposed to, intended to, might wish to, might have occasion to", etc.

Resolve

Résoudre un problème should ordinarily be rendered "solve a problem". According to Webster, *"resolve*, as contrasted with *solve*, is likely to indicate analytic arrangement and consideration of the various phases or items of a problem . . . rather than finding a final solution or answer . . ." etc.

For obvious reasons, "resolution" of a problem for "solution" is a dangerous word to use in conference work.

Resourcefulness

One of the conference translator's most valuable assets is an ability to straighten out loose thinking without departing noticeably from the original and possibly wounding national pride or personal self-respect. Consider the sentence: *"Un Etat Membre doit aussi veiller à suivre une politique conforme aux obligations que la Charte lui inspire."* If this is translated more or less literally, a certain illogicality appears which is not so apparent in the French; after all, a State is under no obligation to follow any policy at all. In a curious way, without saying it in so many words (". . . *doit s'assurer que la politique qu'il suit est conforme . . ."*), the French sentence seems to imply this. But it is hard to feel that the translation is correct unless in the English we put the emphasis in its right place: "A Member State must also see to it that its policy (or the policy it pursues) is in keeping with . . ."

Les problèmes que les peuples ont à résoudre pour construire leur avenir . . . This may be logical to the French mind, but ". . . build their future" begs the question whether the future, once it is theirs, has not already been built. Analogy with "building one's dream house" does not quite remove the doubt (see *Nuance*). But "build a future for themselves" neatly sidesteps the difficulty and is still a real translation.

In a translators' examination which I had occasion to mark, the technical paper described a machine, its parts, etc., and its price *avec un équipement complet.* Most candidates were satisfied with "complete equipment" or "all its equipment". The one generally outstanding candidate had for this "with the full range of accessories".

Restrictif

Une énumération restrictive is a list of the *only* cases, i.e. an exhaustive list.

S

Sabotage

The very different meanings this word can have are worth noting, since ignorance of them has been known to produce a howler. 1. Sabot-making; 2. Chairing (railway term); *table de sabotage* = chairing tread; 3. Bungling, botching (of a job); 4. Sabotage, malicious destruction.

Sacrifice(s) (F)

This word may, of course, mean "sacrifice(s)" in English. But in different contexts it may also mean things as different as "effort(s), concessions, hardship", etc., e.g. *La France est disposée à faire un sacrifice* . . .: ". . . is prepared to go to a good deal of trouble, put itself out."

Saisir (de)

Refer to, lay before, have before (it), submit to, have to deal with, entrust with, cope with, put (place) on agenda. "Seize of" may sometimes have to be used but should be avoided as far as possible. (See *Jargon*.) *La Commission est saisie de* . . .: "The Committee has (had) before it, . . . is (was) asked to consider, . . . is (was) given . . . to study", etc.

Sans doute

"No doubt" (which hardly means more than "very probably") rather than "undoubtedly". Sometimes "probably", "of course", even "perhaps".

Sciences humaines

The social sciences.

Sein

Au sein de la Commission: "in, within, the Committee". With verbs like *choisir*, often "from among the members of".

Sensible (E)

The French word *sensible* does not mean "sensible" in English. It seems elementary to point that out, yet occasionally a translator will commit this schoolboy howler. The French is *sensé* (or *raisonnable*, or one of many alternatives). The French word *sensible*, on the other hand, means "sensitive, susceptible, impressionable", etc. in a human sense; while *sensitif* has the same meaning (sometimes translated as "sensory") in relation to plants, nerves of the body, etc. (See also *Délicat*.) Spanish makes a similar distinction between *sensato* (sensible) and *sensible* (sensitive).

Seulement

See *Only*.

Si

1. A phrase like *Les problèmes des pays sous-développés, si vastes et si complexes* sounds perfectly normal in French; the translation "which are so vast and so complex" has a slightly foreign ring, reminiscent of the tourist's "your so wonderful London policemen". Better say "the extraordinarily wide and complex problems . . . .". If a word like *néanmoins* occurs in the second part of the sentence, the first part might be translated ". . . vast and complex though they are . . .".

2. The concessive use of the conjunction *si* is much more common in French than that of "if" in similar circumstances in English. In a sentence like "If I seem unenthusiastic, it is not because I disapprove", there is a suggestion that I may or may not be; but there is no such latitude in *"Si mon pays est membre du Comité, c'est parce que . . . ."*. The country obviously *is* a member. In general, it is preferable in translating such sentences to avoid using "if". There are various devices that can be used. "The reason why my country . . ." ". . . explains why my country . . .", etc.; and in other contexts "What makes . . . is, . . .; the reason being that", etc.

Situation (F)

"Position" is often better than "situation". e.g. *La situation financière des membres du Secrétariat*: "financial position, condition(s), circumstances, how . . . are placed".

Solidarité

If an expression like "fellow-feeling, community of interests, unity of purpose", etc., will reproduce the precise sense, it is probably better to avoid the very Latin-sounding word "solidarity". "The French origin of the word is frequently referred to during the period of its introduction into English use (in 1848)." (O.E.D.)

Solution (F),

This word often does not really mean "solution" at all, but rather, the means of arriving at a solution, i.e., "course, method, approach, procedure, how to solve", etc., e.g. "It was the duty of all States which were genuinely in favour of peaceful solutions to make their voices heard." (Solutions to what? Since the context does not refer to anything in the nature of "problem", "solutions" here presumably means "a peaceful outlook, the peaceful settlement of differences".) *Aussi bien dans la littérature que dans le domaine des solutions pratiques.* Not "solutions" But "practical achievements".

Solution of, to, for
   The following is suggested as a useful rule-of-thumb: *"The solution of a problem"* But *"a solution to (for) a problem"*, e.g. "holding up the solution of the problem"; "to seek a solution to (for) the problem of". In the former example "the" solution implies something which can be visualized; "a" solution is still hypothetical.

Solve
   See *Resolve*

Souligner
   French précis-writers appear to draw more or less indiscriminately on a whole series of verbs — ostensibly meaning different things — to avoid the monotony of introducing speakers' remarks with the verb *"dit"*: *fait observer, rappelle* (see *Rappeler*), *note, déclare, explique, souligne, annonce, constate, précise,* come at once to mind. To translate *souligner* as "underline" or "emphasize" may suggest a conviction, vehemence or force that was in fact wholly absent. Indeed, French revisers dislike the word anyway.

Souple
   Flexible, adaptable, elastic, . . . allows some latitude, etc.

Spécialisé
   Translators might well consider the possibilities of the word "specialist" used adjectivally as an alternative to "specialized", which sounds odd in certain contexts, e.g., *cadres spécialisés*:

"specialist staff" rather than "specialized staff". "Skilled, highly skilled, technical" are other possible translations.

Specific

This valuable omnibus word would be more valuable still if its use in translation was reserved for occasions when no other word will fit. Translators are urged to try other words before falling back on it.

Spelling

Translators brought up on the American form of spelling should note one or two general principles of "British" spelling as used in United Nations documents: in words of Latin or Greek origin having "ae" as a vowel, American English usually uses "e" alone, e.g., "pediatrics, archeology". "British" English prefers "paediatrics, archaeology". American English tends to omit the hyphens in compound words; British English tends to use hyphens, e.g. petro(-)chemicals, anti(-)histamine, etc.

Style

The canons of English style, like the British Constitution, are largely unwritten and elusive. Writers like Fowler do not and cannot pretend to lay down the law as to how the language shall be used. They merely, or at any rate essentially, formulate principles they deduce from the practices of recognized masters of English writing. All of us who have any pretensions at all to writing well tend to regard ourselves as having a special insight into the secrets of good style. There is no great harm in this, so long as we try not to be over-dogmatic and bear in mind the flexibility and irrepressible pragmatism of English. Perhaps the most dangerous type of "authority" on English style is the grammarian who applies logic or historical evidence in order to produce inflexible rules. The genius of English surely lies in its resistance to rules and its disdain of mere logic. Thus "while" we may argue that "while" is a temporal conjunction and therefore should not be used in the sense of "although" or "whereas," the fact is that good, respectable writers do so use it, and authorities like Gowers and Fowler recognize it.

Similarly, there is an old grammarian's rule that a sentence should never begin with "however". "However", a rapid glance at random through any dozen well-written books will show that this is by no means taboo among recognized writers of pure English. Churchill's genuine or apocryphal "up with which I will not put" has mercifully laughed the taboo on final prepositions out of court. But there is still a great deal of nonsense preached in the name of "correct" English style and usage.

For the conference translator, style must not be equated with elegance. There may be very little time for polishing his version, and the chances are that the original is anything but elegantly expressed. But if this Handbook makes a constant plea for care in the way of handling the target language, it is first and foremost in the interests of lucidity, simplicity and readability. A superimposed veneer of "style" is even less called for in international conference documentation than in most other forms of prose writing.

Submit

A draft resolution should be described as "submitted", not "put forward" or "proposed". The word "presented" may be used of the oral "introduction" of a text which is being formally submitted.

Suivi (le)

Follow-up; monitoring.

T

Tâche

The word "task" in English can sometimes conveniently be omitted and included in the verb. *Confier une tâche à quelqu'un* might in a particular context be best translated as "to request someone to do something". Similarly, *faciliter sa tâche* would be "to help him, make it easier for him . . .", rather than "to facilitate his task". (See *Gallicisms*.)

Technical terms

The language of technology has a dangerous fascination for the layman. It is a sound principle not to use a technical term in a translation unless you are quite sure that it is correct. A more or less literal translation may make the expert smile, but he will have no difficulty in recognizing the sense and mentally substituting the technical term himself, whereas a wrong term may mislead him.

Tendance

Tendency, trend, leaning, inclination, movement, bias, new (change of) policy.

Thanks to

Grâce à (see *Gallicisms*) is more acceptable in French than "thanks to" is in English. If we can substitute the use of "as a result of, because of, with the help of, through, by means of", etc., the translation will probably be the better for the variant.

Thèse

Argument, theory, principle, contention, theme, topic, what . . . trying to prove, etc. Avoid "thesis" if possible.

This and that

Conference translators and précis-writers grow so accustomed to avoiding "this" when translating or producing précis that they tend to use "that" in direct speech when "this" would be more appropriate, e.g., *L'homme est infiniment plus complexe que l'installation la plus perfectionnée . . . Cela explique le succès . . .* etc. *Not* "That explains" *But* "This explains", or "which explains".

That

Are we to say "Mr. JONES (United Kingdom) said that

he would . . ." *or* "said he would . . ."? Translators and précis-writers are sometimes puzzled by the lack of uniformity among revisers on this point. The question is of course largely arbitrary. *Hansard* and *The Times* parliamentary reports ordinarily omit the "that". But there is something to be said for it on grounds of euphony and sentence-rhythm where another "that" does not follow immediately, e.g., "*Mr. JONES* (United Kingdom) said that his delegation was in favour of . . ."; *But* "*Mr. JONES* (United Kingdom) said he would prefer that the . . .".

Tiers monde

A few years ago, when this term first appeared in international conference vocabulary, it was regularly translated in a political context as "the non-aligned, uncommitted countries". The third world is now an accepted term, like "developing countries", which has superseded the other versions with slightly condescending or pejorative overtones: under-developed, under-privileged, etc.

Tourisme

Unfortunately the ugly word "tourism" is now firmly ensconced in international life and language, and there is no way of getting rid of it. Expressions like "tourist trade, tourist activities" may afford a slight relief.

Transaction (F)

A "*faux ami*". Often means "compromise" rather than "transaction"—though of course it can also mean this.

Translatorese

Many of the following examples (not necessarily all to be denounced out of hand) involve a sort of "word fascination", the tendency to provide every word in the original with an equivalent word in the translation. Some of the examples illustrate the fact that it is very easy, and all too common, for anyone translating or speaking foreign languages constantly to grow so familiar with the foreign turn of phrase that a literal rendering into English sounds right.

Les préoccupations . . . sont bien fondées. Not "well founded" *But* "justified, there is (was) some point to, there are (were) grounds for".

Not "The problem was one of how to attain that goal" *But* "The problem was how to . . .".

. . . ne pas participer aux élections prévues pour 1965, élections imposées par . . . Not " . . . not to participate in the elections scheduled for 1965, elections which have . . ." *But* " . . . scheduled for 1965 and made necessary by . . ." (or, if causality is implied ". . . since they have been made necessary by . . .").

Les tribunaux peuvent valider un mariage. Une autre raison justifie une telle position. Not "There is another reason for this position" *But* "There is another reason for this" (see *Position*).

Elles peuvent invoquer les dispositions législatives. Not "the provisions of the law" *But* "the law".

La première de ces différences tient au fait que . . . Not ". . . relates to the fact that" *But* ". . . is that . . .".

. . . les tristes moments que les colonisateurs belges les ont obligés à vivre . . . Not (surely!) "the unhappy moments which the Belgian colonizers forced them to live" *But* "the hard times (hardships) which . . . forced them to endure".

On est d'accord pour reconnaître que . . . Not "All were agreed in recognizing that . . ." *But* "All were agreed that . . .".

La dernière question est celle de la coopération. Not ". . . is that of cooperation" *But* ". . . is cooperation".

La question de savoir si. Not "The question as to whether" *But* "The question whether . . ." or simply "Whether".

"Apartheid was inhuman; but it was also paradoxical in the present situation of South Africa. That country was in a state of full industrial development." Revised version: "Apartheid was not only inhuman, it was also paradoxical in . . . South Africa, a country . . .".

Passant à l'examen de l'amendement. Not "turning to a consideration of the amendment" *But* "turning to the amendment".

Dans les intérêts bien compris des utilisateurs. Not "in the interests, properly understood, of the users" *But* "in the best (real) interests . . ."

Exploiter une mine, une entreprise. Not "exploit a mine, an undertaking" *But* "work a mine, carry on an undertaking";

Les renseignements qui se trouvent à la page . . . *Not* "the information appearing on page . . ." *But* "the information given . . .", or simply "the information on page . . .";

Sa délégation a demandé . . . *cette position est conforme* . . . *Not* "That position" (q.v.) *But* "That was in keeping with . . .", or "The request was";

M. X n'accepte pas ce point de vue. Not "did not agree with that point of view" *But* "did not accept the argument" or simply "did not agree";

Il ne partage pas l'avis de ceux qui estiment que. Not "He did not share the views of those who thought that . . ." *But* "He did not share the view that . . .";

Cette expérience montre que l'exécution de la courte peine peut se faire sur des bases rationnelles où le souci du reclassement social est prédominant sans pourtant énerver la répression puisqu'aussi bien une place suffisante y est laissée à l'intimidation. The following translation (not doctored in any way) is surely unintelligible: "The experiment demonstrates that short sentences can be executed on a rational basis, where concern for the offender's social rehabilitation predominates, without however weakening the repressive aspect, since sufficient room is also left for deterrence." Revised version: "The experiment demonstrates that the enforcement of short sentences can be rationalized so as to throw the emphasis on social rehabilitation, without weakening the repressive value of the penalty, since the importance of a deterrent is not overlooked."

Il lui est impossible de souscrire à la déclaration du représentant de la France qui a dit que . . . *Not* ". . . who had said that . . ." *But* ". . . the statement by the French representative (to the effect) that . . .";

. . . *veiller à ce que cet apport n'entraîne pas de bouleversements regrettables sur le marché. Not* ". . . does not bring about

80

a regrettable disruption . . ." *But* ". . . does not have the unfortunate effect of disrupting . . ."

A literal rendering of the pluperfect in French sentences may produce ponderous or Gallic English: *Not* "thanked the Conference for having elected him" *But* "for electing him"; *Accusait l'Administration d'avoir encouragé. Not* "of having encouraged" *But* "of encouraging". (See also *Faciliter, Si, Gallicisms,* and other examples *passim.*)

Transport

Un transport: a haul, transport operation, consignment, shipment.

Tribunal

Note that the ordinary word for "law court" in French is *tribunal* rather than *cour,* so that the translator should think twice before translating *tribunal* as "tribunal". But note: *tribunal arbitral* = arbitration (arbitral) tribunal, and there are many other instances where "tribunal" is meant. (See also *Valeur* below.)

Trip

Do not speak of a Visiting Mission from an important international organization, or a journey or tour by a technical assistance expert, as a "trip", unless the text is deliberately trying to point out the triviality or uselessness of the travel undertaken, which is not usually the case.

V

Valeur

Cet argument prend toute sa valeur si l'on se rend compte . . . Not "acquires its full value" (see *Translatorese*) *But* "can be best appreciated, is seen in its proper perspective, can be assessed at its true value, the force of this argument can be seen from . . .",* etc. Note also *Tribunal des valeurs,* the French title of what in Egypt is called (in English) the Court of Ethics.

Vocation
In addition to the ordinary meanings: "calling, bent, inclination, being cut out for", etc., there is a slightly different connotation which is more and more frequently found in international conference language, e.g. *Mon pays a une vocation industrielle:* ". . . has an industrial future, is well endowed to become . . ., has . . . possibilities, has prospects as . . .", etc.

Voeu
Recommendation, wish, hope, desire.

Voie diplomatique
Those who regularly use this means of communication—and they ought to know—seem to prefer "the diplomatic channel" to the plural form.

W

Whose
. . . *actions dont les conséquences:* "Actions whose consequences"? or "Actions of which the consequences" or "the consequences of which"? Most writers on English usage appear to agree that the taboo against "whose" with an inanimate antecedent merely makes for stiffness and pedantry.

Word order
See *Paraphrasing.*

NOTES

NOTES

NOTES

NOTES

NOTES

NOTES

NOTES

NOTES

NOTES

NOTES

PART II

TRANSLATING FROM SPANISH INTO ENGLISH

Part I of this Handbook, originally constituting the whole of it, is for convenience entitled "Translating from French into English". In actual fact it deals also, in many of the longer headings, with general principles of translation applicable to translation from or into any language, and these are summed up in the Postlude: "The Elements of Good Translation" at the end of the volume. Cross-references to these general headings are given where appropriate in Part II, and the reader is urged to refer back to the principles involved and to adapt them, *mutatis mutandis*, to Spanish-English translation.

A major problem for the translator from Spanish who has to deal with international organizations documentation is that there are twenty-odd Spanish-speaking countries, each with its peculiarities of usage, in some cases wide differences of vocabulary and syntax, and words and expressions that have very different meanings. Indeed, many of the entries in this Part II contain linguistic forms which make educated Spaniards — who like the British in relation to the English language tend to regard themselves, rightly or wrongly, but understandably, as the guardians of "their" language — throw up their hands in horror. The fact remains that there are at least twice as many Spanish speakers in Latin America as in Spain, and the international conference translator is likely to be faced with the Spanish of the Americas far more often than with Iberian texts. Anyway, whatever the source of a document for translation, and whether it is written well or badly, the translator still has to translate it, and it may be some consolation to the neophyte to learn that an old stager like myself, who has translated for the international organizations from fourteen languages, still finds Spanish, especially that of Latin America where he lived for a number of years, one of the most difficult of all languages to render satisfactorily into English.

Important Note

The following abbreviations are used throughout Part II: As in Part I, the words *"Not . . . But"* are not intended to be categorical. They must be judged in the context of the terms discussed. The letters (E), (F), (Sp), (Port) following a heading are used to distinguish words spelt the same in two or more of the languages. References to dictionaries (q.v.) are given as follows:

(BD) = *Beyond the Dictionary in Spanish;*

(Coll) = *Collins's Spanish — English English — Spanish Dictionary;*

(DA) = *Diccionario de la Real Academia Española,* 1970 edition;

(Mol) = María Moliner: *Diccionario de uso del español,* 2 vols.

(S & S) = *Simon & Schuster's International Dictionary,* English/Spanish, Spanish/English, ed. Tana de Gámez (see Part II: *Dictionaries*).

Other dictionaries are referred to by their full titles.

A

Abocarse

El Comité se abocó en la discusión; después se abocará a la tarea . . . The dictionaries have "meet, have an interview with," etc. but give little indication of the sense "embark on", which is clearly what it means here.

Abordaje

The dictionaries give only "the act of boarding a(n enemy) ship, etc." but the word seems to have been used recently as a Spanish equivalent of the neologism "approach". *"Abordar"* is of course commonly used in the sense of "to approach

96

(someone with a suggestion)", "to take up" (*abordar un asunto*), so that the extension is understandable. Semi-technical or jargon words of this sort often turn out to be attempts to translate English neologisms in a variety of ways (see *Follow-up*).

Acciones

Certain words can be used readily in English in the plural in one particular sense, but not in another. "Actions speak louder than words" is unexceptionable; but "health actions" for *acciones de salud* does not sound right. In this phrase the word means "operations, schemes", and should be so rendered, or according to the context as "types of action". In the WHO Regional Office for the Americas the official version of *acciones de salud* is "health activities", although *acciones* is more concrete, more circumscribed, than *actividades*.

Actitudes

See Part I: *Attitudes*.

Acueducto

Water main, conduit, water supply system, pipeline. "Aqueduct" suggests a large-scale channel or "aqueduct bridge".

Adecuación

Upgrading, updating, refurbishing, keeping abreast of events, overhauling, adapting, fitting in, adjusting to match, etc. In view of the vagueness of the term, and with the advent of forms like *macroadecuación*, it might be well to fall back on the perfectly good if somewhat unfamiliar English word "adequation". In a United Nations document, the term "modernization of the Administration" was translated into Spanish as *adecuación administrativa*. Occasionally used in the sense of "reform".

Adelantar

"To make headway with", hence "to pursue" and hence simply "to carry out, conduct" (e.g. *adelantar una*

97

investigación). The idea of progress has tended to become blurred, cf. "go ahead with", "develop" (q.v.).

Adiestramiento

See *Training*. There are many words in Spanish to express the general idea of "training": *capacitación, preparación, adiestramiento, entrenamiento, perfeccionamiento, enseñanza, instrucción,* are some of the others. These are gathered together under the entry *Training,* where an attempt is made to sort them out.

Administración

According to the context: the Administration, the Government, the Establishment, the Civil Service, the authorities, etc.

Alguno

Spanish seems to be more and more reluctant to use the word *ninguno,* and the use of *alguno* instead can lead the translator astray. *No hay duda alguna* has the negative to indicate fairly clearly that the meaning is "there is no doubt whatever". Now look at the following, translated from English, so that the meaning of the original is perfectly clear: *el Secretario advirtió que si alguna de las alternativas era operable . . . Not ". . . if any of the alternatives . . ." But:* "if *none* of the alternatives . . .". Good Spanish would say *si ninguna . . .,* but the translator has to render what is written, good or bad.

Another tricky use of the word is seen in the following sentence: *Se reservó la posibilidad de hacernos llegar alguna sugerencia de detalle. Not ". . .* a suggestion on a point of detail" *But* ". . . the odd suggestion; one or two suggestions".

Alteración

Like *altération* in French (q.v.), the word frequently has pejorative overtones: deterioration, change for the worse. In medical texts "upset, degeneration, deterioration, worsening (in the) condition, pathological change" might give the correct interpretation. A satisfactory general equivalent might be "disturbance". The word also has several other quite different meanings however: altercation; commotion; vexation.

Alternar

The word normally means "to alternate, take turns". But note the following sentence: *Es importante que los alumnos ciegos alternen en la escuela con alumnos videntes.* Not "alternate with" but "mix with, fraternize". In Spain the hostesses in bars *alternan* with their clients. They are even called *"chicas de alterne"*.

Although

Spanish — and indeed other languages too (see Part I: *Si*, para. 2) — often leaves the force of a conjunction or word performing that function to be determined according to the context. *Habiendo 25 escuelas de medicina, solamente dos de ellas tienen hospital propio.* Here the *"solamente"* gives the clue: "There are 25 . . . but only two . . ." or "Although there are 25, only . . .". The same construction in another context could merely mean "while, as" (cf. the Chilean folksong *"Anoche estando durmiendo, me vinieron a avisar . . ."* "Last night as I slept . . .").

Ambiguity

See Part I: *Ambiguity*. Here are two Spanish examples taken from professionally translated texts:

(a) *Permite asimismo promover la especialización necesaria.* Not "It also makes possible promotion of the specialization necessary" (which is quite ambiguous) But "makes possible *the* promotion . . ." or "makes it possible to promote the (degree or type of) specialization necessary".

(b) *Debe reconocerse que una cierta proporción de tales hogares pueden estar perfectamente contentos"* Not "It should be recognized that to some extent such households may be . . ." But "that a certain proportion . . . may be" ("to some extent" could refer to *all* households).

América

The peoples of Latin America regard this term as including

themselves, without the necessity for qualification. An easy way out in translation is to call it "the Americas". Spanish-speakers refer to what we would call "Americans" as *Norteamericanos* (see BD, *norteamericano,* for an interesting article on the term). For translation purposes, the "North" should ordinarily be omitted when the context indicates that "U.S. citizens" are meant. Where Canadians are included, "North American" is clearly in order in certain circumstances. (See also *Estados Unidos.*)

Amiguista
A word not found in the dictionaries: "fellow-traveller". The usual word is *simpatizante. Amiguista* can also have the sense of "favouring one's friends, resorting to nepotism".

Analizar
See Part I: *Analyse* (E), where the entry would apply equally well to Spanish. "Discuss" would often be a satisfactory rendering of *analizar.*

Anglicisms
The marked tendency for the world's main languages to take over words and their meanings from English does not constitute any special problem for the English translator. The word *ignorar* (or *ignorer* in French) may not appear in the best dictionaries except as meaning "not to know, to be ignorant of"; but in "international conference" Spanish fairly frequently, and in French just occasionally, the word may wrongly but clearly have the sense of "ignore, disregard". Cf. also *"el potencial — o definido — incremento"*: clearly "definite". The translator should naturally be on the look-out for this kind of misuse of the source language. (See also *Causa; Decolaje; Eventualmente; Gallicisms.*)

Anteprima
The titles, etc., preceding the signature of a document.

Anticipar
Can mean "to pay in advance", and even "to promise, state

in advance, pledge". *El estado anticipa el estipendio de los becarios, pagándolo mensualmente.*

Aparecer

Often means "to be" rather than "to seem to be". *La deficiencia nutricional aparece como el más serio problema*: "turns out to be, is, constitutes, the most . . .". (See BD, p.115.)

Apartado

Among the many meanings of this word (see S & S) is that of "Box No.", "P.O. Box" (also *caja postal*). But sometimes it is used as "chapter, main section or even subsection, subparagraph (of a book), title (of a legal document)", etc. Another sense is found in *apartado de los toros*: selection of bulls by separation from the herd, to be sent to the bull ring —not, perhaps, a connotation likely to occur in international conference work.

Aprendizaje

The commonest meaning of this term nowadays is not "apprenticeship", which is a somewhat old-fashioned concept, but "learning" or "the learning process" (*aprender*). *Enseñanza y aprendizaje* = teaching and learning.

Aprobar

Note that in Spanish resolutions no distinction is made as a rule between "approve" and "adopt". The difference in United Nations usage is that a measure or resolution is "approved" by a subsidiary body and subsequently "adopted" by the parent body. (See also BD, p. 13.)

Arrestado

The usual word for "arrested" is *"detenido"*. The term *arrestado* implies "jailed", not merely "taken to the police station".

Articulación

Often = co-ordination.

Asamblea
   Estado de asamblea: state of alert.

Así
   BD gives a longish article under this heading. The following additions may be useful. (1) I would say that *a las seis o así* is less usual than *a eso de las seis*. (2) More interesting, though not usual, is an expression like *Se indican, pues, como sujetos de la rehabilitación vocacional los mayores de 17 años, así adolezcan de limitación visual congénita*. The subjunctive makes it clear that *así* here is the equivalent of *aunque, ya sea que* = "even though". S & S gives *iremos así llueva* = we will go even if it rains, in the same sense. *Así que venga* = as soon as he arrives.

Aspecto
   Here are some examples additional to those in Part I: *Aspect*, including *en este aspecto* = in this respect. *En algunos aspectos puede paliarse esta falla. Not* "in some aspects" *But* "in some instances". *Hubo avances en aspectos relacionados a la preservación*. Since this is the first sentence of the passage, *aspectos* cannot refer to anything that has gone before. ("Aspect" in English cannot usually stand by itself. Aspect of what? one asks.) Here: "areas, matters". Heading of a questionnaire: *Aspectos específicos sobre las preguntas*. The word *sobre* makes it quite clear that it does not mean "aspects of". From what follows it is certain that the meaning is "Special points concerning". Even the word *específicos* can hardly be translated literally — which illustrates an important principle in translation. The purpose is to render the *thought* expressed in the original. One of the translator's tasks is, judiciously and within limits, to make the writer make sense even when he misuses words. A useful word for giving the force of this word *aspecto* is "factor".
   Another example: *Se han abierto halagüenas posibilidades para la utilización del espacio cósmico . . . Este es el grandioso aspecto positivo" Not* "This is the grandiose positive prospect" *But* "This is the positive (q.v.) outlook, and an impressive one it is."

B

Barriada, barrio

Barriada is a word used in many Latin American countries for "shanty-town" (q.v.). *Barrio*—suburb, like *suburbio* (see *Shanty-town*)—seems to be losing social status, and unless qualified (e.g. *Barrio Alto*) may well suggest the poorer quarter of a town.

Bases

The word is sometimes used in the sense of "the grass roots, the rank and file": *las bases del partido optaron*.

Beneficencia

Public Welfare, as distinct from Social Security. These are highly important organizations in the Latin American countries. The term can of course also refer to private charity.

Binomio

"Binomial" is a word hardly used in English outside the sphere of mathematics. DA gives it only in that context. But I have seem the word used to describe the national electoral slate—"Presidential and Vice-Presidential candidates"—and no doubt its use will be extended further to give a pseudo-erudite cachet to ordinary matters. "Twin candidates" (Presidential candidate and his running mate—United States), "names bracketed together", are possible ways of rendering the term. (See also *Fórmula.*)

Biunívoco

Correspondencia biunívoca: one-to-one ratio or correspondence.

Brillante

See Part I: *Brillant.*

C

Cabildo

The regular meanings are "city hall; town council,

ecclesiastical community" or meetings of these bodies. The sense seems to be extended further in expressions like *cabildo abierto* (open discussion) and still further to mean simply "parleying, talks". *Cabildear* is "lobbying" (with a suggestion of questionable behaviour).

Calificar de

"Describe as, refer to as, dub, speak of as, deem". "Qualify" virtually never.

Campo

In international conference work, this word is more likely to refer to the rural areas of Latin America or "the camp", as the non-urban area is called by the English-speaking colony in Argentina, rather than to "countryside", which suggests English cottages with roses round the door.

Canalización

In a medical context: "referral" (of cases).

Cancelar

DA gives only the sense of *anular, hacer ineficaz, borrar, abolir, derogar*. A common use, both in Spain and in Latin America, is "to settle, pay off". Thus *cancelar una deuda* is not to waive or write off the debt, but to pay it!

Canciller, cancillería

Perhaps the commonest use of these words is to translate "Minister and Ministry of Foreign Affairs" (U.K. *et al.*), "Secretary of State and State Department" (U.S.A.). There are of course many other uses to be found in the dictionaries, such as the "Chancellery" of an embassy or consulate, the *canciller* being the chief officer in charge.

Capacitación

See *Training*.

Carrera

Carrera universitaria could mean simply "university career", from freshman to emeritus professor. Frequently it refers to the regular undergraduate course leading up to a professional degree, and should be translated accordingly. (See also BD.) *Todas la carreras de la salud*: all the health professions.

Catamnesis
See *Follow-up*.

Causa
Planificar con mejor conocimiento de causa: ". . . with a greater understanding of the forces at work". See Part I: *Cause*. The Spanish expression would seem to be adopted from the far more common French expression: *en connaissance de cause*. (See Part II: *Gallicisms*.)

Circunstancia
Esta circunstancia, junto al hecho . . . It is not necessary to say "This circumstance, combined with the fact that . . ."; in ordinary simple English we would normally say "This, combined with . . .". (See also Part I: *Translatorese*.)

Coincidir en
Less likely to mean "coincide with" (= *coincidir con*) than "have a bearing on, parallel, dovetail, etc.".

Comisión
Sometimes used in the sense of "squad, team". *Comisión de rescate* = rescue team. What we would call a panel is at times referred to as a *comisión*, perhaps to avoid the word *panel*, which is an Anglicism in this sense.

Como
BD gives a number of useful expressions under this heading. One use likely to mislead is illustrated in the phrase . . . *aparecen algunas opciones de política económica como son el.* . . . A translator with a fair knowledge of Spanish wrote ". . . appear, as do also . . ."! It means simply "such as".

Competencia

Often "sphere of influence, purview, jurisdiction, context, beat". Also, of course, "competition".

Comprender

Comprendo (or *entiendo*) *la preocupación de aquellos que* . . . We do say "I understand your position"; but in certain contexts it may be well to indicate in translation that the sense is not so much "comprehend" as "understand and appreciate". If this is quite clear, "appreciate" or possibly even "sympathize with", in a given context, might render the original thought more accurately.

Concentración

Can mean a mass meeting or (political) rally.

Condiciones

Carece de las condiciones necesarias: "is not equipped for, not qualified for, not in a position to", etc.

Confrontation (E)

The word *confrontación* in Spanish has a rather more bellicose connotation than the English cognate. *Controversia* and *enfrentamiento* would ordinarily be rendered as "confrontation", and "challenge" might be a better rendering of *confrontación*.

Consecuente

Normally "consequent", but may also mean "subsequent", without any suggestion of cause and effect.

Consolidación

In the language of GATT, and no doubt of other organizations, *consolidación arancelaria* is "tariff binding".

Consultar

Este programa consulta la colaboración en el desarrollo. "Has to do with, concerns, involves, provides for" is the sense. *Los diversos temas que consulta el cápitulo* might be translated "The various items coming under or within, included in, embraced by, constituting, the chapter". The word is tending to be used as a synonym for *contemplar*.

Contado

A translator with an indifferent knowledge of Spanish might well make a howler by confusing *de contado* = at once, on the spot (see also *Rato*) and *al contado* = in cash. Note also *contadas páginas*: (a) few pages. *Contados son los países que tienen* . . . "Very few countries have . . .". Note also *por de contado* = *por supuesto* = obviously; of course.

Contradictorio

Like *contradictoire* in French (q.v., Part I), this word has a special meaning in legal terminology. *Procedimiento contradictorio* and *interrogativo contradictorio* involve confrontation with a witness, or in U.S. practice "adversary proceeding". The general Spanish dictionaries have little to say about the use of this term, but Harrap's French dictionary has a useful article on the subject, and the legal dictionaries naturally give it.

Control posterior

Follow-up (q.v.).

Convencional

There is much more often in Spanish (and indeed in French: *conventionnel*) than in the English cognate the notion of "agreement" as opposed to the extended notion of "usual, commonplace". Hence "by agreement, agreed, contractual" may be preferable to "conventional". Occasionally, the word has the pejorative sense of "by underhand agreement", *sub rosa*, cf. *nivelación convencional de precios*: "collusive price-fixing".

Conveniente

"Appropriate, suitable, desirable, advantageous, relevant to, consonant with", rather than "convenient".

Cooperar
"Co-operate" suggests a certain equality between the parties. "Assist" is often better.

Corolario
Occasionally used in an attempt to translate "follow-up" (q.v.).

Corporación
In addition to the sense of "municipality", this word may have the more abstract sense of "municipal government". It can also mean organs of public law such as professional colleges.

Corresponder
Me corresponde a mí: "It is my turn, responsibility, concern; it is up to me." *No me corresponde*: "It is no concern of mine; it is not for me to . . ." More generally, "be in keeping, in harmony with, play the part of, match".

Costeable
Previo estudio de factibilidad, se decidió que el proyecto era costeable: "Following a feasibility study, it was decided that the scheme was economically viable." "A sound proposition" would be another translation; also "cost-effective".

Coyuntura(l)
Elementos coyuntrales: economic factors. *La coyuntura* is the economic situation at a given time. "Cycle, cyclical" will sometimes fit the context.

Criollo
The word is obviously the cognate equivalent of "creole"; but words of this kind should be used with circumspection in international organization texts. The tendency of terms indicating or suggesting family or ethnic background (*castizo, indígena, lugareño* are others) to acquire a pejorative tinge in this or that country prompts caution. *Criollo* usually means

108

"of Spanish descent but born in Latin America", or at any rate "of genuine Latin American stock". Thus the term has a healthy, vigorous connotation which "creole" no longer has —apart from the fact that, in America at least, the word today has colour implications that are best avoided. Perhaps the safest approach is to keep the word *criollo* in translation, and to qualify it where appropriate, in parenthesis, as "(of European origin)", "(authentic Latin American)", etc.

Cuadro

In medical terminology, *el cuadro de una enfermedad* means the "clinical picture, disease profile, clinical chart". Sometimes its meaning is clearly "symptoms, conditions" or simply "the disease, the illness". *Cuadros tóxicos*: toxicity phenomena.

Cuarto intermedio

An odd expression which I have not found in any dictionary. *En régimen de cuarto intermedio*: during the recess period, in the coffee break. *La Asamblea pasa a cuarto intermedio*: The meeting went into recess. The more usual formula in Spanish is: *Se suspende la sesión*, and in English "The meeting is (was) suspended".

Cuota

Una multa de doscientas a quinientas cuotas (Cuba) would appear to be a fine equivalent to the stated number of unspecified units of payment, presumably differing according to the economic ability of the person incurring the fine to pay, e.g. a day's wages, a percentage of net worth, or some such unit. "Personal payment unit" or simply "quota" (which leaves the sense unclear) are possible translations.

Chabolismo

Shanty-town life, the shanty-town problem. (See *Shanty-town*.)

D

Dead Wood

It is a well-known fact that a passage in French or Spanish and the same passage in English, whichever was the original, will be some 10-15 per cent shorter in the English version. The main reason is that the Latin languages often add words for colouring or for stylistic reasons, and also that these languages do not lend themselves to cutting corners in the same way as English does. Cf. *La educación del pueblo se presenta como un componente indispensable.* The idea implied is "proves to be, manifests itself as, is seen to be", but in English these are all too strong, and the most satisfactory rendering would probably be "Educating the public *is* an essential component". A sentence like *"En lo que se refiere al informe, éste constituye la prueba . . ."* need not necessarily be rendered as "As far as the report is concerned, it constitutes . . ." Since the subject is the report, the sole purpose of the lead-in is to give a slight, and usually unnecessary, fillip so that the change of theme, or the subject word, is slightly stressed. Unless the context suggests that a parenthetical "of course, after all, on the other hand" is latent, the phrase is probably best rendered simply as "The report constitutes the proof . . ." or at most "The report itself . . ." (See Part I: *Resourcefulness*). Turning language which for either personal or national reasons the writer feels the need to round out with comfortable flesh in order to make it read well, into the kind of English that will not strike the English-speaking reader as fulsome or overblown, is a subtle exercise in psychology as well as a linguistic task. Other examples of this characteristic feature of unimaginative translation are given in Part I under *"Translatorese"*.

Decolaje

The ordinary word for the "take-off" of an airplane would be *despegue*. The use of *decolaje*, a word of which all the dictionaries I know are innocent, illustrates the usefulness of knowing other languages. The word is clearly a Gallicism: *décollage* is the regular term in French for "take-off".

Defensa

In translating this word, the translator would do well to consider whether "safeguard" would not read better than "defence" in the particular context. (See also *Garantía*.)

Deferencia

La deferencia que se sirva dispensar a este asunto . . . A translation revised by me read "Any courtesy you may wish to extend to this matter . . ." It is first of all nonsensical, since the courtesy would be extended to the persons concerned; secondly, the politeness is rather nauseatingly gushing in English. "Any action you may (kindly) see fit to take in the matter" is more sober, better English, and closer to the emotional level implied in the Spanish.

Derecho positivo

See Part I: *Droit positif*.

Derivaciones

Las derivaciones de una política: the consequences or outcome of a policy.

Desarrollar

The phrase *desarrollo de actividades de investigación* in a context which indicates that hitherto there has been no *investigación*, suggests "The organization (introduction, initiation, institution) of research". International affairs jargon not only encourages Spanish speakers to misuse the word *desarrollar* in this way; it also gives its blessing to such terms as *desarrollo de una política*" or "development of a policy" where no "further" action is implied and the meaning is clearly "formulation, fashioning, building up from scratch." Webster gives no sanction for the use of "develop" in the sense of "start up, install, organize". A useful way out where the sense is not

111

clear is to translate as "promote", which can have both meanings.

Deteriorar
According to the dictionary, in English the word "deteriorate" can be both transitive (= make worse) and intransitive (= grow worse); but in general usage only the intransitive use is found. In Spanish "*un factor que deteriora la salud*" is quite normal. "Impair, undermine, upset, aggravate the health situation" may fill the bill in a given context.

Determinar
. . . *énfasis en actividades que determinen los cambios* . . . "Determine" will not quite do. "Activities which are responsible for, cause, condition, are the determining factor in, bring about . . ." This use, which is very common, is not mentioned in BD's article on the word.

Diagnóstico
"Diagnosis" in a non-medical context borders on jargon. "Assessment; long, hard look; review of the situation; overview", etc., may be better.

Diciente
Exactly parallels the word "telling" in English, in the sense of "striking, significant, eloquent".

Dictar
Dictar un curso, una conferencia: to give, conduct.

Dictionaries
For some strange reason, Spanish has fared much less well than French, Italian, German and several other European languages in the way of dictionaries. The standard Spanish/Spanish dictionary is the *Diccionario de la Academia*, in which most translators into Spanish seem to place blind trust. It is woefully conservative, and of relatively little use for translating modern, technical, or Latin American texts.

112

Much more useful among unilingual dictionaries is Moliner: *Diccionario de uso del espanol*. The system of ordering within each heading is odd and rather complicated, but it is much more up-to-date and therefore in many ways of more practical use to the English translator than the Academy dictionary. The best Spanish-English bilingual dictionary I have seen at the time of writing is Simon & Schuster's *International Dictionary E/Sp—Sp/E*. The next best is probably *Collins's Spanish—English English—Spanish Dictionary*. The *Larousse Spanish—English English—Spanish Dictionary* is almost as good in its way as either. None of these is nearly so good as the best French, German, Italian, Dutch, Swedish bilingual dictionaries. But they are a distinct improvement on Appleton/Cuyás, Cassell, Michaelis, Amador, etc.

For the clarification and discussion of terms that go beyond the scope of even the best Spanish dictionaries there is an excellent little book which takes precisely these words for its title: *Beyond the Dictionary in Spanish*, by A. Bryson Gerrard (Cassell)*. It is aimed essentially at those interested in acquiring a more profound knowledge of Spanish rather than at those concerned with translating the language, and hence the peculiar problems of translation are generally outside its scope. But "BD", as I call it, is referred to frequently here in Part II, and users of this Handbook are strongly recommended to obtain it. As regard technical dictionaries, the best-known general works are Sell's *Comprehensive Technical Dictionary* (McGraw-Hill), out-of-date but useful; Robb's *Dictionary of Legal Terms* (Wiley & Sons); the Spanish edition of *Dorland's Illustrated Medical Dictionary* (the standard American work on the subject); and Elsevier's multilingual dictionaries, which cover a vast variety of technical subjects and at least sixty of which include English, French and Spanish, are indispensable aids to this aspect of translation.

Difundir

Spread, disseminate, make widely known, publicize, apply on a broad scale, etc.

---

* A revised edition of this book has now been published, under the title of "*Cassell's Colloquial Spanish*, in England by Cassell and in the U.S.A. by Macmillan. For convenience, the abbreviation "BD" is retained here in all references.

Disponer

BD has a good article under this heading. "Dispose of" meaning "have at one's disposal" is a *"faux ami"* perpetrated constantly in English by foreigners. Germans in particular tend to use "dispose of" (or "over") for *"verfügen über"*. Where *dispuesto a* equates fairly well with "disposed to", it may be advisable to clarify still further and say "willing, ready to".

Distensión

A Gallicism (q.v.) replacing *relajamiento de tensiones*, to render the term *détente*.

Dotación

Ordinarily "endowment", etc.; but cf. *tener una sede en la cual pueda desempeñarse la dotación permanente del Comité* . . . its regular membership. *Dotación de personal*: staff, establishment, strength, crew (of a ship), etc. *Dotar* is used nowadays, by a strange historical inversion of roles, in the sense of "to make a settlement" (*dote* = dowry) on a wife on entering into a contract of marriage.

E

Efectivo, eficaz, eficiente

The distinct meanings of these three words correspond largely to their English cognates; but they tend to be rather loosely used, and as always, the translator must seek the meaning demanded by the context in which the particular word is used.

Elementos de juicio

See Part I: *Eléments d'appréciation*.

Empleado, -a

Generally "salaried worker, employee, white-collared worker", as opposed to *obrero*: "manual worker, blue-

114

collared worker", etc. In Spanish America, the words are also used for "(man)servant, maid, char". (The word *"empregada"* in Portuguese almost invariably has this meaning.)

Enganche

Coupling, hitch. By extension, enlistment in the armed forces. *Banderín de enganche*: recruiting post. In a slightly colloquial context, the word can mean a "down payment".

Entrenamiento

One of the many words for "training" (q.v.).

Enviado

Envoy, messenger, delegate. *Enviado de prensa*: special correspondent.

Equívoco

Note that in South American Spanish this word is sometimes used in the sense of *"equivocado"*, i.e. "wrong", not "ambiguous". S & S calls this use archaic, but it is certainly not rare. AD does not mention it at all.

Erradicar

El municipio hace esfuerzos para erradicar a los ocupantes ilegales de edificios: ". . . is trying to evict the squatters."

Esperar

The fact that *esperar* can mean both to hope and to expect can create problems for the translator. As a rule the particular sense is clear from the context, but where it is impossible to be sure, the translator may have to resort to the old trick of steering a middle course and avoiding the issue. *Estoy esperando el fin*: "I await the conclusion." The word "trust" has an element of both hope and expectation, and will be found useful. BD has a good article under this heading.

Estados Unidos

It may be a wise precaution at times in translating Latin

American documents to adopt the practice common among inter-American organizations of adding "of America" when "Estados Unidos" means the U.S.A. Mexico is officially *los Estados Unidos Mexicanos*" (The United Mexican States) and the assumption that the U.S.A. is meant in any context may give rise to ambiguity or at the very least to hurt sensibilities.

Estamento
This word, used formerly for the "Estates of the Realm" of Aragon, is extended nowadays to mean "social class", "population group".

Eventualmente
There appears to be a tendency today for this word, meaning "possibly, in certain circumstances, as and when", etc. (See Part I: *Eventuellement*), to be used in the English sense as meaning "eventually". Cf. ". . . *problemas que eventualmente dan origen a programas. Una vez logrados, estos programas* . . ." This use is no doubt an Anglicism, but the translator has to cope with it. Expressions like "leading up to, making for, calculated to result in" may be ways of dealing with the point without actually using the word "eventually". (See *Anglicisms*.)

Evolución
In most contexts "evolution" will not be appropriate. "Trend, development(s), future course, way in which the situation is likely to evolve, course of events, outlook", etc. may suit the particular context better.

Excepción
Note the legal sense of "stay, demurrer". *Estado de excepción*: state of emergency.

Extensión
Remember that this word can have two distinct meanings. In the phrase: *La extensión del foco de oncocercose* it means "the extent, the magnitude, of the area covered by" the disease. In another context it could mean "the spread" of oncocercosis.

116

Extremo

A judgement of the OAS Administrative Tribunal uses this word in the sense of "provisions, stipulations, requirements": *Según ese extremo del Reglamento. Extremo* in the sense of "point, issue, question" is fairly common (see Collins's dictionary).

F

Facilitar

To avoid "facilitate", which smacks of translatorese, try "provide, furnish, make available, further, promote, prepare the way for, back up, give a boost (fillip) to", etc.

Facultativo

El criterio facultativo sobre los estudiantes toxicómanos. A trap for the unwary. The word *estudiantes* gives the clue. It means the views of the university faculty!

Fecundidad, fertilidad

According to the United Nations *Multilingual Demographic Dictionary*, the meanings of these words in English are reversed. *Fecundidad* = fertility (the capacity to bear children); *Fertilidad* = fecundity (the size of the family, etc.). This would appear to be the authoritative distinction adopted by population experts; but it must be said that the distinction is not universally observed.

Fibra química

Man-made fibre.

Fiscal, fiscalizar, fisco

These are words that give translators a great deal of trouble. *El fisco (Fisco)* is the Treasury. The adjective *fiscal* is therefore used in the same sense as "fiscal" in English, e.g. the fiscal year = the financial year. It can also mean simply "governmental";

fiscal is an inspector, supervisor, and (with a capital F) the Public Prosecutor (U.K.) and the District Attorney (U.S.A.) (also called *Ministerio fiscal* or *Ministerio público*). *Fiscalizar* is in general "to check", "investigate", "supervise", but it can also mean to collect taxes, and to criticize or censure. The difficulties are compounded in French, where the word is mainly concerned with taxes and taxation. *Le fisc* is the Exchequer, the Inland Revenue authorities. (See also Part I: *Ministère public*.)

Filiación
Parentage, family background, as part of *Generales* (q.v.). In law, legal parentage, filiation.

Follow-up
This convenient term has not yet found a really neat equivalent in Spanish, either in its medical meaning or as a general term. In international organization documents I have had to deal with, all the following expressions were more or less successful attempts to translate the term "follow-up": *catamnesis, control posterior, corolario, estudio de casos* (*clínicos*), *observación ulterior de casos, seguimiento, tratamiento complementario, vigilancia ulterior*. (See also the word "*preservacão*" under "*Portuguese (Translating from)*".)

Formación
See *Training*.

Fórmula
The slate, ticket, list of candidates in an election. *Compañero de fórmula*: running-mate. (See also *Binomio*.)

Frente a
"In the face of, when faced with, in confrontation with, when confronted with, in the light of, in view of, as against, as contrasted with, etc."

G

Ganadería

Cattle-raising, cattle-rearing, stockbreeding, animal husbandry, ranching, livestock-farming, etc. These terms mean much the same thing, but local or national usage, and common sense, will usually dictate the appropriate term in a given context. "Animal husbandry" is a useful neutral term. *Agricultura y ganadería* is often best translated simply as "agriculture" or "farming".

Garantía

See Part I: *Garantie*. "Safeguard" will usually be better than "guarantee".

Generales

Personal data, *curriculum vitae*.

Generalidades

Like "generalities" in some English expressions, this word tends to have a pejorative connotation, indicating or suggesting a superficial approach to a problem.

Graciable

Pensión graciable: *ex gratia* pension.

Guaraní

Not all Paraguayans are ethnically *Guaranís*, but the word is sometimes used meaning simply "Paraguayan".

Gallicisms

See also Part I: *Gallicisms*. Translators may find themselves puzzled by a term not readily found in a Spanish dictionary which a moment's reflection will show to be an adaptation from the French. Iberian Spanish is more prone to borrow from the

119

French than the Latin American forms of the language. (See *Causa, Decolaje, Distensión,* etc.)

H

Hacienda
A word with a variety of meanings: 1. Farm, ranch, landed property. 2. Cattle. 3. Finance (*Ministerio de Hacienda*); personal property (*vida y hacienda*: life and property). Note sense 2 in particular. It can prove very puzzling. *Hacienda en pie* = cattle on the hoof.

Harmonizar
Sometimes "co-ordinate, bring into line".

Howlers
In a handbook designed for professional translators, it should hardly be necessary to point out the following, culled from a variety of sources: *cada vez mayor* means "bigger and bigger" and *Not* "bigger each time"; *restar* does *Not* mean "to remain", *But* to "take away from, deprive of"; *recién en 1980* does *Not* mean "recently in 1980", *But* "only in, not until"; *da lugar a* means "gives rise to, provides an opportunity for, etc." and *Not* "accounts for"; *un criterio más* means one more factor or principle, *Not* "more than a principle"; *refrigerio* (q.v.) does *Not* mean a refrigerator but a snack.

I

Ignorar
No self-respecting dictionary gives anything but "not to know, to be ignorant of" for his word. But there is a distinct tendency for the Anglicism to be used in Spanish, in the sense of "to ignore, disregard".

Implementation (E)

The Spanish word requiring this as a translation will probably be *ejecución*, sometimes *implementación* (!), an unfortunate Anglicism; but note that *ejecución de un programa* should be "execution, carrying out", etc., not "implementation". This word has tended to be loosely used. A recommendation is implemented, a programme is executed.

Implicar

Often "involve" or "entail" rather than "imply", e.g. *El decreto implicará la convocatoria a la Asamblea*: *Not* "shall by implication convene . . ." *But* "shall involve the convening . . .".

Impresionante

Not "impressive" *But* "alarming", "sobering," "startling", etc., as a rule. *Quedé impresionado* I was moved, shocked, startled. (See BD: *impresión*.)

Inconsulto

High-handed(ly), without consulting anyone, decided arbitrarily.

Inédito

In the Southern Cone countries of South America at least, this word is commonly used in the sense of "unprecedented, unheard of, novel, innovative" rather than in the literal sense of "unpublished".

Influjo

This word is sometimes used in the sense of *influencia*, cf. *al influjo de un mejoramiento de los términos de cambio* "under the influence of . . .". Spanish speakers frown on this use, but recognize that it is not uncommon.

Inquietud

A popular word today among the intellectuals of Latin America in the sense of "intellectual curiosity, concern for what is going on in the world", etc. In political speeches, "progressive outlook, open-mindedness, liberal philosophy, enlightenment" may render the idea satisfactorily. *La colaboración que Ustedes nos entreguen será de enorme valor para nuestras inquietudes*: ". . . valuable in helping us to solve our problems, a valuable contribution to our efforts, . . . in satisfying our sense of curiosity, of value to our thirst for knowledge, . . . to us in our anxiety (eagerness) to learn", etc.

Insistir
See Part I: *Insister*.

Integral
Atención integral del diabético: comprehensive care of the diabetic. The word sometimes appears to be used in the sense of "integrated (with)", and vice versa, *integrado* can be synonymous with "integral", i.e. complete, comprehensive.

Integrity of the sentence
It has been indicated more than once (See Part I: *Paraphrasing*) that too liberal an attitude towards the shape of the original text can quickly make translation degenerate into paraphrase. Perhaps a sound criterion in approaching a sentence for translation would be *Not* "How would I myself have couched the thought expressed here?" *But* "How does the English language tend to handle this kind of thought?" cf. *En 1973 se notificó un caso de cólera, cuyo origen no pudo precisarse y que no logró difundirse*. If this sentence is translated more or less literally, the relative will almost inevitably give it a tang of translatorese (q.v.). Here is a case where the Latin preference for a neatly rounded sentence is best matched by the English preference for simplicity and lucidity. Break the sentence into two: "One case of cholera was reported in 1973. Its origin could not be traced, and the disease did not spread."

Intendente
Provincial Governor (Chile); Mayor (Argentina). In Spain,

a general in the Quartermaster Corps. *Intendente de 2ª*:
Brigadier in the Q.M.Corps; *Intendente general*: Lt.-General
(ditto).

Intensificar, intensivo
Acción intensiva: vigorous action. *Se intensificará la
necesidad de capacitación de personal . . ."* The need . . . will
become more acute, will be felt more acutely". "Intensify" is
a word rather to be avoided as introducing emotive overtones
where they are not called for.

Interiorizar
Digest, absorb (ideas). "Internalize" has good credentials,
and is used frequently in sociology and psychiatry; but in non-
technical texts it is perhaps too reminiscent of what the lion
did to young Albert.

J

Jornada(s)
The frequent use of this word nowadays (usually in the
plural) in the sense of "symposium, seminar, workshop, (short)
practical course" is, unaccountably, not given in any of the
dictionaries I have consulted.

Juridicción
Juridicción contencioso-administrativa: Tribunal for (the
settlement of) administrative disputes, or the system of
administrative challenge. It is not always clear in a given
context whether *juridicción* is concrete (the court or tribunal)
or abstract (the system), or merely "jurisdiction" in the sense
of competence to deal with a matter.

Jurisprudencia
Case law rather than jurisprudence, which in English has
a wider, more philosophical connotation. *Jurisprudencia
constante*: the settled practice of the courts.

L

LAB

Not always recognizable as the Spanish equivalent (*libre a bordo*) of f.o.b. or FOB (free on board).

Licenciado (F. licencié)

It is the practice in the United Nations — and a sound one — to ignore attempts to extend handles to people's names by calling them Ing. Fulano de Tal, Lic. Machinchose, etc. These, along with Ph.D.s, are simply called "Mr.". The practice, common enough in the United States, of using the word "ambassador" as a title: "Ambassador Young", for example, was successfully resisted in the United Nations until a year or two ago, when a directive from a source that could not be challenged overruled the would-be guardians of the language.

The title of *licenciado* is approximately the equivalent of "Bachelor (of Arts)". In Mexico, the term is usually applied to the holders of first degrees in law, or simply means a lawyer.

Liderizar

A brave if somewhat unpleasing attempt by a Spanish translator to render the almost equally unpleasing neologism "to spearhead".

Liquidación

An unexpected technical use of this word is found in customs terminology: "assessment" of duties, etc., and in public finance law "determination of the exact amount due or charged".

M

Major (E)

Like *mayor* (Sp. — q.v.), this word may be used in a

124

context where it is not really a comparative, since it is not "compared" with anything. The exact parallel in English would be "superior". If this will not fit, some alternatives are "choice, above average, preferred, especially good, improved", all of them giving the idea of "better", without saying better than what. One thinks of the language of TV commercials: "X gives you more . . .", or of "The Better Gowns department" of a store.

Mandatario

The terms *Primer mandatario, Segundo mandatario* for President and Vice-president, are common enough. Less common is *mandatario regional, provincial, seccional* for governor of a region or province.

Manejo

This word appears to be used more and more frequently — though it is frowned upon by many people — as a Spanish translation of "management" where no "handling" or "manipulation" is implied. *Manejo de especies silvestres* = wildlife management.

Mansión

The dictionaries give "mansion", but not the sense implied in *Le deseo una buena mansión en mi país* — just "a pleasant stay"!

Marginado

Deprived, disadvantaged, marginal, urban-fringe (population groups), etc. Where the word refers more specifically to persons living on the outskirts of cities (and by implication disadvantaged), "urban-fringe population" or even "slum dwellers, shanty-town dwellers" may give the sense. (See *Shanty-town*.)

Más o menos
    See Part I: *Plus ou moins.*

Mayor (Sp)
    BD has an interesting article on this word, but it makes no reference to a very common use of the word, meaning "extremely large, very large, major". A Spanish translation of the two phrases "Special attention will have to be given to" and "The need for major treatment programmes" reads *"se deberá dar mayor atención al problema de . . ."* and *"la necesidad de mayores programas de tratamiento . . ."*. These examples show how ambiguous the sense can be.

Mecanismo
    "Machinery, mechanism, device"; sometimes "organ, agency".

Mediterráneo
    Translators are occasionally caught out by this word. *"Bolivia, paś mediterráneo"* can hardly be anything but "land-locked".

Mexico (E)
    See *Estados Unidos.*

Ministro, Ministerio
    See Part I: *Ministre, ministère.* The same care must be taken. Note, incidentally, that in Italian, ministry is *ministero*, which adds to the possibility of confusion.

Modalidad (-es)
    Like *"modalité"* in French, this word is translated more and more frequently in international conference prose as "modality", a word otherwise little used in current English. "Way, ways and means, device, form(ula), method(s), approach" are possible and usually preferable alternatives.

N

Nacional
Very often better not translated as "national", which may have political overtones, or may be simply meaningless or misleading in the context. *Vestidos nacionales* = clothes of domestic manufacture. *Programas nacionales* = country programming. *Especialización nacional*: *Not* "national" *But* "specialization in the various countries", etc.

Negro
As in the expression *mercado negro*, this word is sometimes used as meaning "illicit, unlawful, underhand", e.g. *migraciones negras* = clandestine migration. Note also *aguas negras*: sewage.

N.M.F. (N.m.f.)
Abbreviations can cause problems in the absence of a good dictionary of abbreviations, of which there are several. None I have seen gives this one = *nación más favorecida* (most favoured nation). English also uses M.F.N. or m.f.n.; French does not appear to abbreviate the term.

Norma, normativo, normalización
"Norm" is a word that strikes a slightly pedantic note in English. Better are "rule, standard", or in some contexts "yardstick, measure, gauge". *Normas vigentes*: rules in force. The *Organización Internacional de Normalización* is the International Organization for Standardization. The word "normative" is so seldom used in English that the average educated person would be at a loss to say what it means. The stock translation of *normativo* is "law-making", but where "law" would not apply, "decision-making, which establishes standards or patterns, standard-setting, regulatory", etc. might serve, e.g. *las unidades normativas del sector salud*: "the decision-making units . . ."

O

Obrar

The idiomatic expression *obrar en poder de alguién* is not given in most dictionaries, and is usually mistranslated for that reason. DA for once scores here: *El expediente obra en poder del fiscal* = simply "is in the possession of, is being handled by".

Observar

In a translators' examination, several candidates read the phrase *la necesidad de observar la marcha del plan* in an English way and mistranslated it as to "maintain the tempo of . . ., keep the plan moving". This would imply something of an Anglicism in the use of *"observar"*. The sense is "to follow the progress of the plan". *Observar* can also mean "to respect" (the law), "to comply with, implement" (a resolution).

Ocasión

Para ser publicado en la ocasión de la reunión. In certain contexts it may be well to avoid "on the occasion of", which may suggest "at the time of, contemporary with". "In connection with", which may mean before or after, may take care of the ambiguity.

Ofrecer

The word "offer" in English usually implies an option to decline what is offered. But not always: "offer a sacrifice, offer (up) one's prayers" means "to give, present to". Spanish and Portuguese seem to have extended this usually religious sense, and a Brazilian will say "I offered my daughter a new dress for Christmas", meaning "I gave to, bought for, presented to". "Provide with" may sometimes be a good rendering.

Oleaginosos

The general term used, e.g. in GATT, is oilseeds, though

strictly it should include oilseed cakes and meal. Spanish uses *semillas oleaginosas*.

Oneroso
Translators familiar with French will note that the frequent use of *onéreux* in the sense of "costly", or simply "against payment" has its counterpart in Spanish, in addition to the usual meaning, "burdensome, onerous"—the latter also in the legal sense.

Oportuno
Timely, well-timed, seasonable, opportune, appropriate.

Orgánico
Ley orgánica: basic, organic, constituent law, "Constitution" of a country.

Orientación
See also Part I: *Orientation*. Other useful if slightly jargon-sounding words would render, e.g., *la orientación y contenido de la asistencia técnica*: "the thrust, the angle, guidelines for", etc.

P

Paralizar
El gobierno paralizó las negociaciones. The word here has much the same force as "to freeze" in English; "suspended, halted, held up" might also be used. *Paralizar las pasiones*: pour oil on troubled waters.

Parte
There is something vaguely wrong with the translation of a sentence like *la parte del poliéster en el consumo mundial de los textiles* as "the share of polyester in world consumption of textiles". The old problem of subjective and objective genitive comes up again, and even if we can hazard a guess

as to the meaning, there is a lurking sense of uncertainty as to whether polyester is being shared out. Better be explicit: "the share (or proportion) represented (or constituted) by polyester . . .". *Por otra parte*. (See Part I under the heading *Part*.) "At the same time" will often translate the expression.

Partera

In countries which are trying to expand their medical and paramedical resources, use is being made of the lay midwives who have traditionally taken charge of childbirths, in rural districts especially. They are given simple technical training, and a measure of status as *parteras empíricas* or "traditional birth attendants" (TBA).

Percepción

Usually means "collection" (of taxes, etc), but in Argentina (and no doubt elsewhere) it may mean a rough tally, rapid check, rule-of-thumb calculation: *una percepción de morbilidad total hecha muestra que* . . . "a rough survey . . .".

Perfeccionamiento

It is sometimes difficult to distinguish the meaning of this word from the many other terms that express the idea of *training* (q.v.). "Continuing education, updating of skills or qualifications, refresher courses" may be helpful. In certain instances "improve and perfect" may give the idea better than either word taken alone. *A medida que este método se generalice y se perfeccione*: "As this method becomes more general and more sophisticated." Other versions of the verb form: polish, refine, mature.

Personería

A slightly less formal synonym of *personalidad* in the legal sense of "status" (as agent, etc.).

Personero

Spokesman, mouthpiece. Also "dignitary".

Peso ley

This term is used in Argentina together with $ and MN (*moneda nacional*). For obvious reasons it is desirable in translating into English to avoid using the symbol $ for any currency other than the U.S. dollar ($US or US$). Even the Canadian dollar tends to be written out in full to avoid confusion. The Argentine, Mexican or other peso is probably best called precisely that, whatever the sign or abbreviation used in the original, and $J may not be readily recognized as the Jamaican dollar, unless the context makes it perfectly clear.

Peste

La peste is "the plague", in the medical sense, e.g. *peste bubónica*, whereas *una plaga* is "a pest", e.g. *plaga del jardín*: garden pest. But usage is not so straightforward. *Una plaga de langostas* = a plague of locusts, but *una peste de ratones* = a plague of mice. *Peste aviar* is fowl pest. There are also many other uses of both the words, and several standard dictionaries have good entries under these headings.

Plantear

One of the notoriously most difficult words to translate into English. DA defines the word as "*Tantear, trazar o hacer planta de una cosa para procurar el acierto en ella*. S & S has: 1. To outline, set forth, state, expound. 2. To raise, pose (problems, doubt, question); to propose, put forward (solution, etc.). 3. To establish, set up, put into operation. Other possibilities are "postulate, theorize, speculate", and for the noun *planteamiento* "premise, exposition, assumption, proposal". It should be noted that the word *planta*, with its many and various senses, from "plan" (blueprint) to "plant" (factory), is at the root of the words.

Plantel

Personal de plantel: regular staff, permanent staff.

Plática

Normally "a chat". A prisoner *en libre plática* is one allowed to receive visitors, i.e. not incommunicado.

Plazo

Some suggestions: term, period, timetable, time schedule, time scale. Note also *pagar a plazos*: pay by instalments, *comprar a plazos*: buy on credit. In certain contexts, may also mean "time-limit, deadline".

Pliego

Strictly a folded sheet, but by extension simply "sheet of paper, section of a newspaper, schedule". *Pliego de condiciones*: specifications, list of conditions; *pliego de costos*: bill of costs. Other meanings are given in S & S.

Polivalente

Polyvalent, multivalent, broad-based, all-purpose, versatile. (As a noun:) Jack-of-all trades, generalist (all according to context).

Ponencia

Ordinarily "report, statement", but in Spain the word can also mean a "panel" set up to report. (See also *Comisión*.)

Porque, por que

Verbs like *velar por* have given rise to a construction not easily found in the dictionaries, and not particularly good Spanish. *La labor del servicio es velar por que* (sometimes wrongly written as *porque*) *se tome en cuenta*: "to see to it that . . ." A similar construction is found with verbs that do not so regularly have "*por*" e.g. *La Organización tratará por que se obtenga subsidios*: ". . . will try to arrange for".

Portuguese (Translating from)

This heading is not quite so out of place as it may seem in a section devoted to translating from Spanish. Translators with a good knowledge of Spanish perhaps too readily assume that

132

all they need is a dictionary to tackle anything that comes along in Portuguese.* Spanish is, of course, half the battle; it is the other half that raises the problems, and they can be quite tricky.

The main difficulty is the old *"faux ami"* — the same word or expression in one language meaning something different in the other. This very sentence contains a perfect example: In Spanish *". . . algo distinto en el otro idioma"*. But *". . . que significa uma coisa distinta no outro idioma"* would in all probability mean "something distinguished". The trouble is that *distinto* actually can mean "distinct, separate, different, well-defined". But the ordinary word is *diferente*, and *distinguido* means "differentiated", not "distinguished" in the sense of "eminent", which is the ordinary meaning in Spanish.

Here are a few other words that can easily mislead translators of Portuguese who know only Spanish:

Constante. Os números constantes da lista acima. Not "The constant numbers of the above list" *But* "The numbers comprising . . ."

Extensão. See *Extensión* in the Spanish glossary.

Nesta. No Portuguese dictionary to my knowledge gives the very common use of this word meaning "local(ly), here in this town". In Rio de Janeiro, *"Ilmo. Sr. João Pereira da Silva, Rua do Ouvidor 20, Nesta"* would mean residing here in Rio. Spanish says *"presente"* or *"plaza"*, but this normally implies that the communication is delivered by hand (*en manos*).

Para o inglês ver is *Not* "To see the Englishman", *But* "For the Englishman to see", "To show the British (what we can do)"—an allusion to the traditional local envy of the British engineers, etc., who worked for a long time setting up the Brazilian railways about the turn of the century, and the determination to go one better.

Personal infinitive. Translators who assume that they can guess Portuguese if their Spanish is good can be caught out by this peculiarity of Portuguese. The following translation shows how. *Seria tolice perdermos tempo discutindo os*

---

* Perhaps I should establish my own credentials by saying that I lived for several years in Brazil.

133

méritos . . . This was translated as: "It would be foolish —
in fact we are wasting time discussing . . . " The translator
here has obviously assumed that *perdermos* is a misprint
for *perdemos*. The correct translation goes quite neatly into
English: "It would be foolish for us to waste time. . ."

Pesar. Cf. *Em todos os paises, em que pesem os esforços
realizados pelos* . . . This is a curious, somewhat archaic
expression found both in Brazil and in Portugal, with an
unexpected meaning: "in spite of the efforts made . . ."

Ponta (da). Cf. *Punta* in the Spanish glossary. *Da ponta* is
short for *da ponta da orelha*, literally "of or from the lobe
of the ear". Anything that is excellent is described *"da ponta"*,
the person taking the lobe of his ear between the thumb and
forefinger. If the thing so described is outstanding in its
excellence, it may be described as *"da pontinha"*, in which
case the arm is extended above the head so that the thumb
and forefinger of the right hand hold the lobe of the left ear,
or vice versa. This may seem to have little relevance to
international conference work, but I have actually witnessed
the gesture made in a PAHO (WHO) meeting apropos of
some brainwave issuing from one of the delegations.

Preservação: In disease control, an odd way of saying
"follow-up".

Restar. See this word in the Spanish glossary. In Portuguese
it has the same meaning as in English.

Tesoura. This does *not* mean "treasure" (*tesouro—tesoro*
in Spanish) *But* "scissors" (*tijera* in Spanish).

Positivo
See Part I: *Positive.*

Precario
At times means *Not* simply "in a hazardous position", *But*
actually "poverty-stricken, hand-to-mouth".

134

Preparación
See *Training*.

Presencia
La presencia de una enfermedad: occurrence: See Part I: *Presence*.

Primer magistrado
Like *primer mandatario*, this term is sometimes used in Latin America to designate the President of the country. In many countries, including Spain, he is the Head of State, whether President or King.

Programar
A useful translation is "schedule".

Prolongado
Often "lengthy" rather than "prolonged", which suggests "extended beyond a particular point". See also Part I: *Réduit*, where the problem is the same, as also with *reducido*.

Promiscuo
Of a judge: of mixed jurisdiction.

Propender
El centro propenderá de inmediato a la modificación . . ." *Not* "The Centre will incline forthwith towards making changes" (which is the worst kind of translatorese) *But* "The Centre will take steps at once to change . . .".

Prosecretario
As in English "pro-cathedral", the prefix embodies the idea of "standing in for". Hence "assistant secretary". *Protesorero*: deputy treasurer.

Punta
Sector de punta: the new, advanced, as opposed to the

traditional sector. See also *Portuguese (Translating from)*: *Ponta (da)*.

Puntual

Criterios que podrían ser implementados en forma puntual: promptly, definitely, adequately. Almost synonymous with *de forma cabal, cabalmente*.

Q

Que

Tales casos, desde luego que no son consecuencia de la ceguera, sino el resultado de la carencia de recursos. At first sight, this (complete) sentence would appear to have no main clause. But Latin American Spanish in particular will often throw in a "*que*" which does not introduce a subordinate clause but merely gives a slight impulse to the verb. The translation might be simply "Obviously such cases are not . . ."; but what the Spanish is really saying is: "Such cases—well, it's obvious, of course, that they . . ."

R

Radicación; radicar

Found used in the sense of "submission, filing; to submit, file" (an application etc.) A common meaning is, of course, to settle, go and live (somewhere), cf. *estar radicado en Madrid*.

Rata, ratón; rato

Normally in Spanish, the ending −*ón* suggests increase in size or importance of the word to which it is applied. But note that *rata* = rat, whereas *ratón* is mouse! (cf. also *pelón* =

sin pelo; rabón = sin rabo). Note also *esperar un rato, un ratito* = wait a (little) while.

Razonado

Plan razonado—plan with commentary (cf. *raisonné* in French); *catálogo razonado (catalogue raisonné)*: annotated list.

Realidad

Han definido su política en base al análisis de su(s) realidad(es) nacional(es): ". . . on the basis of the hard facts of their situation as a country; . . . of things as they stand in the country". *Nuestra realidad*: our situation; the position we are in; this milieu. *En realidad* is usually less strong than "in reality". "Actually" is nearer, or omit altogether as a phrase used for padding.

Reducido

La reducida fertilidad de la tierra probably *Not* "The reduced fertility", which would suggest that it was previously more fertile, *But* "The (relatively) low fertility . . .". (See Part I: *Réduit*.)

Referir

Referir los resultados del estudio: Report on, describe.

Refrigerio

Corresponds to "snack" in English. It can also mean, as in Italian, "relief, comfort, consolation".

Refuerzo

Cantidad de refuerzo: supplement, "sweetener", retainer. *Dosis de refuerzo*: booster dose.

Refundido

Lista refundida: consolidated list.

137

Región

In Spanish American texts, *"la Región, la región"* usually means simply "Latin America".

Regular

A notorious pitfall in Spanish. It very frequently means "mediocre, not too good, rather poor", e.g. *el empeoramiento de las ya regulares condiciones del mercado* might be translated as "the worsening of the already rather poor conditions . . ." or "the worsening of the market situation, which was none too lively to begin with".

Restar

Note that in Spanish *restar* ordinarily means "deduct, take away" *Not* "remain, rest" (*quedar, reposar*), though it can have these meanings. In Portuguese the sense is as in English or French.

Resultar

Resulta interesante notar que: *Not* "The result is interesting in that . . ." *But* "It is interesting to note that . . .". There is a colloquial but frequent use of *resultar* in the sense of *"resultar conveniente"*: *resulta viajar en primera clase*: "it is worth while travelling first class", or even "it is fun, it is pleasant, it pays off".

Ritmo

A word commonly used in Spanish and Portuguese, like *"rythme"* in French, in a context where "rhythm" will not do in English. "Tempo" will often serve, although as any musician knows, the two words do not mean the same thing. "Pace, movement, rate" are other useful synonyms.

Ruble

Occasionally found instead of *rubro* (heading, item, rubric).

Rueda

Rueda de la bolsa: "Today's trading on the stock exchange".

Corro is similar in meaning. *Rueda de prensa*: press conference.

S

Sectorial
"Sectoral" rather than "sectorial", when used as the adjective form corresponding to "sector".

Seguimiento
One of the many neologisms used to translate "follow-up" (q.v.).

Sensato, sensible
See Part I: *Sensible* (E).

Sensibilización
El proceso de sensibilización de la sociedad (in relation to environmental problems) might be translated as "arousing public awareness". In other contexts the term is used to translate the "softening-up process". In a technical context (medicine, photography) = "sensitization".

Sentar
El infrascrito senta un recurso contra . . . "lodges (files) a complaint . . .".

Shanty-town
BD gives a dozen words used in Latin America to designate this distressing phenomenon, referred to sometimes as *chabolismo*, from *chabola*: hovel. *Erradicación del chabolismo* is an important aspect of Spain's housing policy. BD does not include the Peruvian euphemism *"ciudades jóvenes"*.

Significar
La dilapidación de recursos que significa repetir trabajos. Notice how the typical inversion here changes the sense.

Not "which means repeating" *But* "which comes of repeating". "Involved in, implied by" will often fit into the context.

Signo monetario
   Unit of currency.

Simplificación
   In a phrase like *simplificación del proceso de aprendizaje,* the neologism "streamlining" may serve.

Simular
   The Watergate cover-up was sometimes referred to as *la acción de simular los hechos.*

Sistema
   This word frequently denotes something less grandiose than "system" implies in English. "Method, scheme, arrangement, device, way of . . .", etc. may render the thought better.

Solicitada
   As a noun = newspaper appeal to voters, political propaganda. *"Solicitación, llamamiento"* are more usual.

Solidaridades
   Mutual interests.

Solución
   See Part I: *Solution* (F).

Soslayar
   Most dictionaries give only the sense of "do or place obliquely". S & S gives the sense of "ignore, evade, dodge". "Circumvent, get round", etc. express the notion of "oblique".

Sueldo, salario
   Note that *salario* is usually "wages" (i.e. daily or weekly payment for a menial task), whereas "salary" (usually monthly remuneration for a skilled job) is *sueldo.*

Superintendencia

The English cognate is seldom used. The Brazilian *Superintendencia do Nordeste para o Desenvolvimento* is officially translated as Northeast Development Authority. But see Part I: *Direction* (F), last sentence.

Superlatives

One of the main reasons why Spanish, especially Latin American Spanish, is described in the foreword to this Part II as one of the most difficult of all languages to translate is because of what elsewhere (see Part I: *Brillant*) is called "the tendency in certain languages to use superlatives, and the consequent need to tone down the language used so as to reproduce the meaning rather than the words".

Su(b)stituir

Ordinarily = replace, *Not* "substitute". *Substituir a por b*: "replace a by b". The word "substitute" here is at best confusing. We would have to say "substitute b for a".

T

Tan

See Part I: *Si* (paragraph 1). *Las ideas tan maravillosas*: "The really (quite) wonderful ideas", or simply "the excellent ideas" (see *Superlatives*).

Tasa

Tasa de . . . por edad: age-specific rate.

Taxativo

Always an awkward word to remember, since it has no easily recognizable root. *Taxis*, in Greek = category. "Specific, concrete, categoric(al); restricted, restricting, limitative." (See Part I: *Restrictif*.)

Tenencia

This term has a variety of meanings: possession, tenure, holding, tenancy, occupancy, lieutenant's functions; post of deputy mayor or alderman; local *carabineros* post or station.

Título

Note among the many quite distinct meanings "titre, or titer" in chemistry; "section, title, part" (of book); "academic degree"; also "title" or "entitlement" in law.

Titular

Note the meanings "headline" (of a newspaper); "chief, head" (of an organization); "holder", e.g. *titular de un derecho* (French = *ayant-droit*).

Toda vez que

A somewhat archaic expression, not to be confused with *cada vez que. Es importante, toda vez que permite comprobar . . . Not* "whenever it allows of" *But* "since it . . ., inasmuch as it . . .". Equivalent here to *ya que; pues.*

Training

It may be useful to try to sort out the many words in Spanish that can regularly be rendered in English as "training". The suggestions for each word must not be taken as necessarily satisfactory in a given context, since the terms are often used loosely.

Adiestramiento implies the imparting of skills: "training, coaching".
Aprendizaje (q.v.) involves the learning process.
Capacitación has the notion of qualifying someone for a particular task: "training, qualification(s)"; occasionally "expertise" (i.e. the outcome of the training exercise).
Docencia is teaching from the point of view of the teacher, or tutoring, instruction (also *instrucción*).

Educación covers the same ground as in English.

Ejercitación refers to the effort made in imparting or absorbing training, indoctrination (but not in the political sense).

Enseñanza would normally be "teaching, tuition", although "training" will often be a more suitable rendering.

Entrenamiento tends to refer to the acquisition of bodily skills (i.e. physical education).

Formación contains the idea of a coordinated effort to fit a person for a task or profession. *La formación general del personal de salud*: training, preparation for the profession. The term is more comprehensive than "instruction", nearer "education".

Perfeccionamiento implies a stage of training further to that already acquired; hence the terms "advanced training, refresher course" (*curso de repaso*) in English are often translated thus in Spanish.

Preparación appears to be a Gallicism in the sense of "training for a career", but it is so used. Otherwise it could be translated as "grooming, briefing".

These terms are often used in the combination: *capacitación y perfeccionamiento*: "training and advanced training"; *formación y adiestramiento*: simply "training" or "training and instruction". It must be realized that many of the words are used more or less interchangeably, so that perhaps the most helpful course will be to give a list of the possible synonyms to be used at the translator's discretion in the light of the particular context: initial training, advanced training, apprenticeship, briefing, coaching, conditioning, directing, drill(ing), education, enlightenment, exercising, further training, improvement of knowledge, grooming, guidance, imbuing with, imparting (of knowledge etc.), indoctrination, instruction, instilling, inculcating, nurturing, pedagogy, preparation (for a career), qualifying, refresher course, schooling, teaching, training, tuition, tutelage, pre-service and in-service training, etc.

143

Other words and expressions likely to be rendered as "training" in English are:

Buque escuela: training ship;

Escuela normal, escuela para maestros: teachers' training school or college;

Escuela práctica: training school (at skilled worker level, sometimes synonymous with

Escuela vocacional: vocational training institution, usually at technical level.

Translatorese

See this entry in Part I. Other examples: *Está de acuerdo con aquellos que piensan . . . Not* "He agreed with the views of those who thought that . . ." *But* "He shared the view that . . .". Good English is much more elliptical than most other languages. Cf. also *El esfuerzo para conseguir tal resultado será árduo Not* "The effort to achieve this result will be" *But* "The effort required to achieve this will be". (See also *Circunstancia*.)

Tra(n)scendental, tra(n)scendente

The philosophical connotation of "beyond the bounds of a single category or of human cognition", which still tends to be attached to the words "transcendent" and "transcendental" in English, likewise exists in Spanish, but the words are more likely to be used in the more mundane sense of "excellent, first-rate, surpassing", and if so they should be translated accordingly. Indeed, the word may hardly be a superlative (q.v.) at all: "important, significant" may be all that is intended.

U

Utilidades

The general word for "profits" of a business, etc. "Utilities" in the American sense of water supply, gas, electricity, etc. would be *servicios públicos (generales)*.

V

Verdadero

Una verdadera planificación intersectorial Not "a veritable
. . ." *But* "intersectoral planning in its true sense, what can
really be called . . .", etc. (Cf. *véritable* in French.)

Versión

Sometimes used loosely as "report", even "rumour". A
common meaning is of course "version, translation" (cf. *The
Browning Version*).

Verter

Sometimes = express, communicate (ideas or opinions to
an organ or agency).

Z

Zootecnia

Animal husbandry (See also *Ganadería*).

NOTES

NOTES

NOTES

NOTES

NOTES

NOTES

NOTES

NOTES

NOTES

NOTES

NOTES

Postlude

THE ELEMENTS OF GOOD TRANSLATION

Reading through the original entries in this Handbook and those of the Spanish Part II, I have reached the conclusion that for the purposes of international conference work, virtually every one of the entries can be subsumed under one or another of a mere handful of guiding principles governing what constitutes good translation. These are given briefly below, unencumbered by references to the text itself, as a tentative decalogue which the reader or school of translation may find comprehensive enough as it stands, or may be tempted to expand into a catechism.

1.   *Meaning.* Good translation of the kind of texts met with in the ordinary way in international conference work attempts first and foremost to render the meaning of the original, the whole meaning and nothing but the meaning, as far as the inherent limitations of language will allow. It guards against the possible accusation that it merely paraphrases the sense; and it neither omits significant elements nor adds explanatory or other matter not included or very strongly implied in the original.

2.   *Form.* It avoids changing the original order of words, phrases or ideas unnecessarily or arbitrarily, i.e. unless the sentence structure of the source language differs from that of English, or unless differences in the way in which the two

languages indicate stress or rhythm make a reshuffling of the parts of the sentence necessary or desirable.

3.   *Idiom.* A good translation into English reads as if it were written originally in English. It does not betray its foreign origin by the way it is written, unless of course by design.

4.   *Mood.* It reproduces or reflects not only the sense but the characteristic mood of the original: solemn or frivolous, earnest or light-hearted, enthusiastic or apathetic, intimate or aloof, imaginative or down-to-earth; and the vocabulary is chosen to match the particular mood.

5.   *Style and clarity.* If the original is stylish and well written, a good translation will have an equivalent style. If it is poorly written, dull, unclear, the translator will take the evident intention of the author for the failed achievement and judiciously clean up the text, brightening it and above all clarifying it, unless of course its defects are deliberate (e.g. politically-inspired obscurity must obviously retain the sibylline quality intended).*

6.   *"Faux amis"* (linguistic). Good translation will be at pains to detect and cope with words or expressions similar in form but different in meaning in the source and target languages.

7.   *"Faux amis"* (cultural). It will avoid terms alien to the culture or environment to which the original refers.

8.   *Jargon.* It will be reluctant to admit popular neologisms, clichés, line-of-least-resistance words, etc.

---

* It could no doubt be argued that the ideal English translation of a bad piece of writing in any language should logically be a bad piece of English; but for the purposes of international conference work at any rate, we need hardly spend time on this kind of sophistry; and if the translation turns out to be an improvement on the original, as it frequently does, it is unlikely that anyone will complain, least of all the author of the original.

9. *Understatement.* Good English translation strives for terseness, concreteness, simplicity of expression, as being notable characteristics of the best English writing.

10. *Primacy of the mother tongue.* Embodying the other nine elements, good translation is the result of the sensitive transference from an original language of which the translator has a sound knowledge into a target language of which he/she has an even sounder knowledge. In other words, since the working translator handling more than one or two foreign languages is hardly likely to have an equal knowledge of all of them, mastery of the source language can never be an adequate substitute for a subtle feeling for language as such and the ability to mould and manipulate the mother tongue as target language with profound knowledge and great resourcefulness.

Postscript to the Postlude

Lest there should be any misunderstanding as to the claims made for the above "principles" ("elements", as I have called them, or even "hints", might describe their purpose better), let me stress the word "tentative" used both in the *Foreword* to this edition and at the head of the *Postlude* itself. If the contents are controversial, as I hope they are, this is in keeping with my intention expressed in the original *Introduction* (see page 12), to be "deliberately provocative", for what seem to me to be the best of reasons.